Rhythm & Rhyme

Literacy Time

1

Humpty Dumpty had a great fall

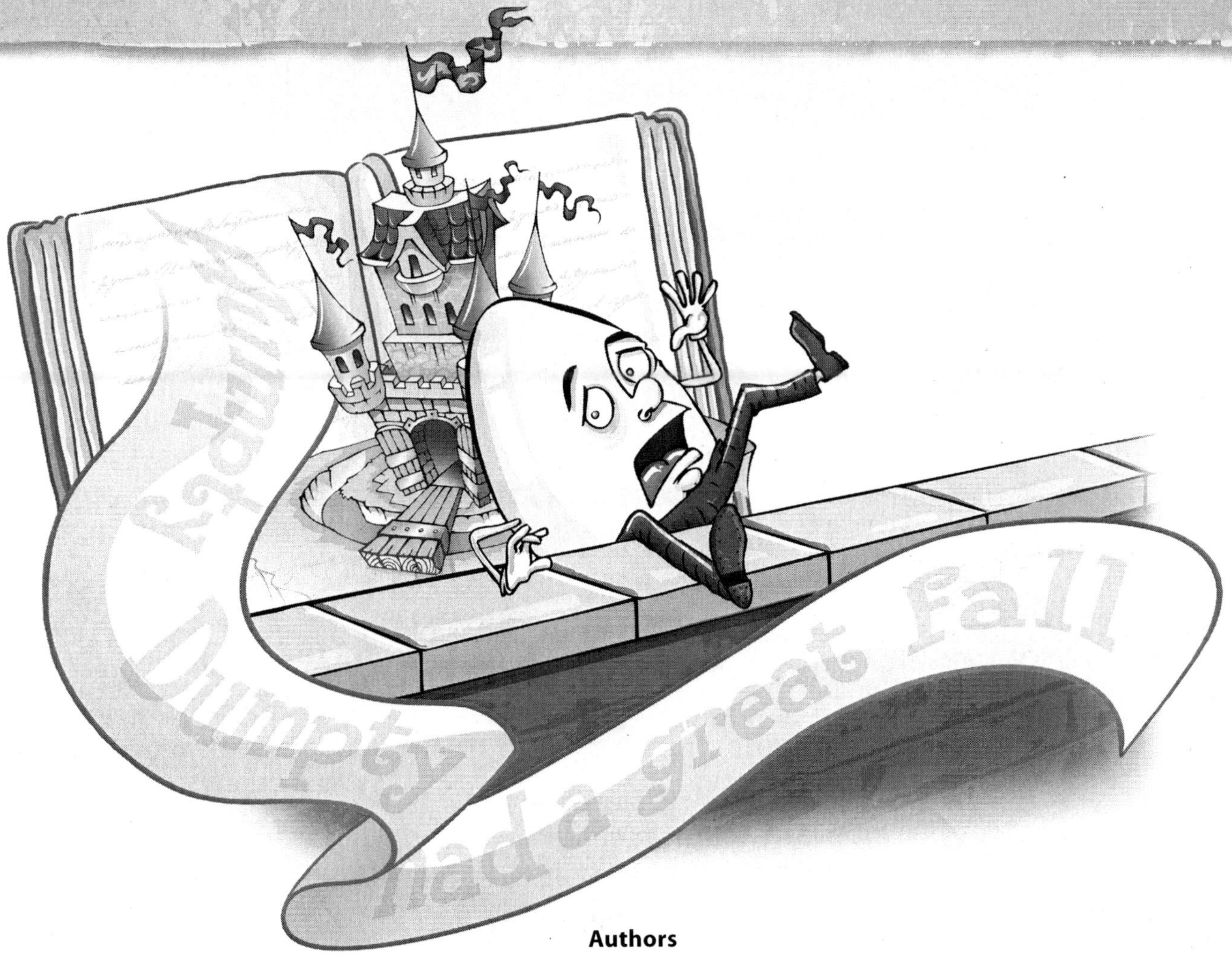

Authors
Timothy Rasinski, Ph.D.
Karen McGuigan Brothers
Gay Fawcett, Ph.D.

Standards
For information on how this resource meets national and other state standards, see pages 139–142. You may also review this information by scanning the QR code or visiting our website at http://www.shelleducation.com and following the on-screen directions.

Publishing Credits

Corinne Burton, M.A.Ed., *President*; Emily R. Smith, M.A.Ed., *Editorial Director*; Jennifer Wilson, *Editor*; Evelyn Garcia, M.A.Ed., *Editor*; Grace Alba, *Multimedia Designer*; Don Tran, *Production Artist*; Stephanie Loureiro, *Assistant Editor*; Amber Goff, *Editorial Assistant*

Image Credits

Dreamstime p. 26, pp. 30–31, p. 57; iStock pp. 4–6, p. 17, pp. 20–22, p. 29, p. 35, p. 37, p. 41, p. 44, p. 46, pp. 49–51, pp. 59–60, pp. 62–63, p. 63, pp. 65–67, pp. 72–75, p. 79, p. 81, p. 85, pp. 97–102, p. 104, pp. 105–106, pp. 112–114, pp. 116–118, pp. 120–122, pp. 124–127, pp. 130–132; all other images Shutterstock

Standards

Shell Education
5301 Oceanus Drive
Huntington Beach, CA 92649-1030
http://www.shelleducation.com

ISBN 978-1-4258-1337-6

Table of Contents

Poetry and Literacy

"Reading should not be presented to children as a chore or duty. It should be offered to them as a precious gift."

—Kate DiCamillo

What better gift to give students than fun rhymes to read in order to build literacy skills? Did you grow up singing a song of sixpence, hoping the kittens would find their mittens, and wondering why Georgie Porgie wouldn't leave those little girls alone? We did, along with generations of children. Mother Goose nursery rhymes have helped children achieve literacy since at least the 18th century. Today, we find that many of our children are missing out on nursery rhymes and poetry. Over the years, poetry and rhymes have been called the "neglected component" and "forgotten genre" in our homes and in our school literacy curricula (Denman 1988; Gill 2011; Perfect 1999). Many teachers think that is a shame, and we heartily agree!

There is a growing chorus of scholars who are advocating the return of poetry and poetry lessons in the classroom (Rasinski, Rupley, and Nichols 2012; Seitz 2013). Moreover, there is a growing body of classroom and clinical research demonstrating the power of poetry in growing readers (Iwasaki, Rasinski, Yildirim, and Zimmerman 2013; Rasinski, Rupley, and Nichols 2008; Zimmerman and Rasinski 2012; Rasinski and Zimmerman 2013; Zimmerman, Rasinski, and Melewski 2013). The following information describes the benefits of using poetry and rhyme to enhance literacy skills in the classroom.

Phonological Awareness

Rhymes provide the context for developing phonological awareness. Dunst, Meter, and Hornby (2011) reviewed twelve studies that examined the relationship between nursery rhymes and emergent literacy skills in more than 5,000 children. All of the studies pointed to a relationship between early knowledge of nursery rhymes and phonological awareness, which is a strong predictor of early reading acquisition (Adams 1990; Ball and Blachman 1991; Griffith and Klesius 1990; Templeton and Bear 2011). In fact, one literacy expert, Keith Stanovich, claims phonological awareness as a predictor of reading success is "better than anything else we know of, including I.Q." (Stanovich 1994, 284). Rhymes provide an opportunity for children to play with words and thus learn how language works (Maclean, Bryant, and Bradley 1987).

Poetry and Literacy *(cont.)*

Phonics

The alliteration of *Goosie Goosie Gander* and the rhyming words of *Jack Sprat Could Eat No Fat* lay the groundwork for phonics instruction. Children can't *sound out* words if they don't hear the sounds. Decades of research have demonstrated that rhymes help children develop an ear for language. In one longitudinal study, researchers found a strong correlation between early knowledge of rhymes in children from ages three to six and success in reading and spelling over the next three years, even when accounting for differences in social background and I.Q. (Bryant, Bradley, Maclean, and Crossland 1989). Poetry and rhymes surround children with the sounds of language—sounds that must be applied in the letter-sound relationships of phonics instruction.

Vocabulary and Comprehension

Even a strong foundation in phonemic awareness and phonics is not enough. Students who can decode words but do not know their meanings usually struggle with comprehension, which is, of course, the ultimate goal of reading. Research has consistently shown a strong correlation between vocabulary and comprehension (Bromley 2007; Chall 1983; National Reading Panel 2000). Typical correlations between standardized measures of vocabulary and reading comprehension are in the .90 or higher range regardless of the measure used or the populations tested (Stahl 2003). Vocabulary development is just one more benefit of using poetry and rhymes with children. Most nursery rhymes present opportunities to learn new vocabulary words that are relevant today but may not be familiar to many six-year-olds (e.g., *fiddle* [Hey Diddle Diddle], *fear* [Three Little Kittens], and *broth* [There Was an Old Woman Who Lived in a Shoe]).

Fluency

The repeated reading of poems and rhymes provides ample opportunities for students to develop reading fluency. Rasinski and Padak (2013) describe fluency as "a bridge that connects word decoding to comprehension . . . Fluency includes automatic word recognition, interpretive and prosodic reading, and appropriate expression and rate. Fluency is the ability to read expressively and meaningfully, as well as accurately and with appropriate speed" (252). Research into repeated readings indicates that reading a particular passage several times, which we suggest you do with the nursery rhymes and poems in this book, leads not only to fluency with that text but also transfers to new, unfamiliar text (Dowhower 1987, 1997; Rasinski et al. 1994; Samuels 1997; Stahl and Heubach 2005).

> "Purposeful practice is essential for improvement and mastery of literacy skills. When given proper instruction, materials, and opportunities to practice and apply what they learn, all students can experience literacy success" (Hackett 2013, 4).

Poetry and nursery rhymes send the all-important message that reading is fun. What children can resist the tickle in their mouths when they say *Fuzzy Wuzzy* or the onomatopoeia of *Baa Baa Black Sheep*? The natural rhythm and meter beg children to recite nursery rhymes over and over, increasing fluency skills more and more each time. Enjoy watching your students light up as they say each and every one of the rhymes in this book.

How to Use This Book

Implementing the Lessons

The following information explains the various activities in the lessons and how to implement them with students. Additional tips on how to implement the lessons, including creating poetry notebooks, can be found on pages 132–133.

Introducing the Rhyme

This section helps teachers introduce the poem to students. Use the steps listed below to introduce all of the poems in this book. Then, continue with the specific tasks mentioned in each lesson.

1. Copy the rhyme on a sheet of chart paper or on the board. (*optional*)
2. Read the rhyme to students using a pointer to track the print.
3. Distribute copies of the rhyme to students.
4. Read the rhyme chorally several times to develop fluency.
5. Have students illustrate the rhyme and add it to their individual poetry notebooks. For more information about how to set up the poetry notebooks, see page 133.

Change a Word

Some lessons include the *Change a Word* activity. With this activity, students are given letter cards (page 134) that can be arranged to make words from the rhyme. **Note:** Some lessons require duplicate letters. Be sure to look at Step 1 in each *Change a Word* activity and write the additional letters on the empty cards. You can also use the blank cards to quickly create new letter cards for students who accidentally lose one of the letters. You may also wish to laminate them for durability. The first word and the last word will be connected to the poem. Sometimes the activity requires simple encoding (using just a few letters to make a simple CVC word chain for the rhyme "Hop, Bunny, Hop": *hop, hot, pot, top, tap, map, mop, hop*). At other times, instructions require students to use the final letter of a word they made to start the next word in the chain (going from *dish* to *spoon* for the rhyme "Hey Diddle Diddle": *dish-hat-top-played-dogs-spoon*).

Since this activity is teacher-led (the teacher reads the clues), it should be done as a whole-class activity, or you may wish to work with some students in a small group. Be sure to clarify any clues or word meanings that students may be unfamiliar with.

How to Use This Book *(cont.)*

Word Ladders

Lessons that do not have a *Change a Word* activity will have a *Word Ladder* activity, which allows students to build and examine words on an activity sheet. To begin, students are given a key word from the rhyme. In order to "climb the ladder," students must follow the teacher's clues and change the first word progressively, thus creating a new word at each step. Clues can require students to add, remove, change, or rearrange letters. The final word relates to the first word. For example, for the rhyme "Fuzzy Wuzzy," students follow your instructions to progressively change the following words: *bear, bar, car, star, stair, hair.*

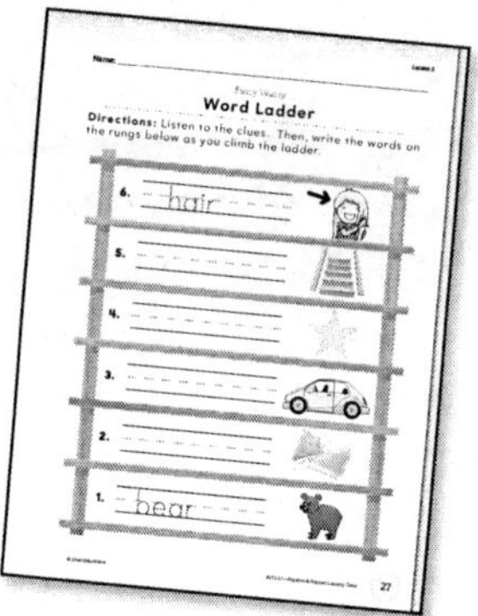

Since this activity is teacher-led (the teacher reads the clues), it should be done as a whole-class activity, or you may wish to work with some students in a small group. Be sure to clarify any clues or word meanings that students may be unfamiliar with.

Word Sorts

The *Word Sort* activity helps students explore relationships among words. Students are given a set of word cards related to the rhyme and work individually, in pairs, or in groups to sort the cards into two or more categories. Some will be *open* word sorts and some will be *closed* word sorts.

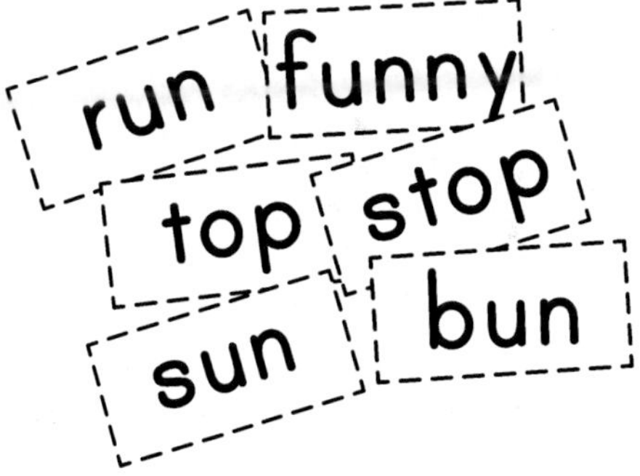

For open sorts, the categories are not predetermined. Students look for commonalities among the words and create their groups or categories accordingly. Then, they share their word sorts with classmates, explaining the groups they created. For example, given a set of picture cards (*skates, sandwich, doll, donut*) students could sort the cards by initial sounds (/s/ or /d/) or by function (toys and food). As long as they can justify their groups, the sorting is accepted. **Note:** You may find open word sorts are effective as pre-reading activities. The sorting allows students to become familiar with the words they will encounter in the rhymes. In addition, the sorting can help students predict what the text will be about. If used as a pre-reading activity, you will want to have them sort again after reading the rhyme in order to see if their categories change.

For closed word sorts, the categories are predetermined. The teacher instructs students to sort their words into specified categories. After the sorting, students discuss the words and why they were placed in the given categories. **Note:** For each closed word sort, we suggest categories for sorting the words. You can also come up with other categories for your students to use.

How to Use This Book (cont.)

Rhyming Riddles 

Each lesson includes a *Rhyming Riddles* activity. Students are instructed to use words in a word bank to answer riddles related to a key word or phrase from the rhyme. Students may be able to do this independently, or it can be conducted as a large group activity. Have students say as many rhyming words as they can to partners before implementing the activity sheets so that students know which rhyming sounds they are focusing on. You may wish to have them use the *My Rhyming Words* template (page 135) to write all of the rhyming words they brainstorm.

Writing Connections

Each lesson includes a *Writing Connection* activity that relates to the rhyme in some way. The activities vary from students writing short, one-syllable words, to writing simple poems, to making lists. We suggest that you use these lessons to generate enjoyment of writing rather than to teach grammar and spelling. Encourage developmental spelling, dictation, and illustrations, and celebrate your young writers' products. **Note**: Have writing paper available for the *Writing Connection* in all lessons.

Reader's Theater

Each lesson includes a *Reader's Theater* script that focuses on the rhyme, where students are assigned parts of a script to read aloud. Oral language fluency is an important precursor to oral reading fluency. Fluent speakers actually help their listeners make sense of words and ideas by speaking at an appropriate pace, using meaningful phrases, and embedding expression and pauses into their speech—essentially the same skills needed for fluent reading (Rasinski and Padak 2013).

Have students rehearse the poem several times by themselves or in small groups to enhance listening and speaking skills and improve students' confidence. Arrange for various ways that students can then perform the poem as well as the accompanying script. Students can perform for classmates, another class, parents, the school principal, other teachers, or even record their reading for later performance. **Note**: There are not enough parts for every student in your class. Be sure to look over the amount of parts before assigning them to students.

All of the scripts provide opportunities for repeated reading, the benefits of which we discussed above. Rasinski and Padak (2013) call it "deep reading" (5) and suggest the following routine: "I'll read it to you. You read it with me. Now you read it alone" (66). The problem teachers sometimes face with repeated reading, particularly with older students, is motivating students to read a text multiple times. As one solution to that dilemma, each lesson has a suggestion for tying the repeated reading to a performance. Students should not be required to memorize the text for the performance but simply be prepared to read it aloud with confidence and with good expression.

Hop, Bunny, Hop

Standards

- Identify words and phrases in stories or poems that suggest feelings or appeal to the senses.
- Know and use various text features to locate key facts or information in a text.
- Decode regularly spelled one-syllable words.
- See Appendix C for additional standards.

Materials

- *Hop, Bunny, Hop* (page 11)
- *Letter Cards* (page 134)
- *Hop, Bunny, Hop Closed Word Sort* (page 12)
- *Hop, Bunny, Hop Rhyming Riddles* (page 13)
- *Hop, Bunny, Hop Reader's Theater* (page 14)

Procedures

Introducing the Rhyme

1. Distribute the *Hop, Bunny, Hop* rhyme (page 11) to students.
2. Ask students to follow along as you read the rhyme orally.
3. Discuss what is happening in each stanza.
4. Read the rhyme chorally several times to develop fluency.
5. Allow students to illustrate the rhyme and add it to their individual poetry notebooks.
6. Have students add the title to their notebooks' tables of contents.

Change a Word

1. Distribute a set of *Letter Cards* (page 134) to each student. If this activity is used early in the year, we recommend you use only the letters they will need (*h, o, p, t, m, a*).
2. Before you begin to play, have students identify the letters and corresponding sounds.
3. Allow students time to arrange the letters to make their own words.
4. After students have had time to make and share words, ask them to put the letters in a pile and follow your instructions to make a word chain from *hop* to *hop* (*hop-hot-pot-top-tap-map-mop-hop*). Say the following:

- We are going to begin by making a word that is in the rhyme *Hop, Bunny, Hop.* Use three letters to make the word *hop.* What letters did you use? Let's say the word and stretch it out.
- Take off the *p.* Put a new letter at the back so that your word means something that can burn you. What letter did you use? (*t*) What word did you make? (*hot*)
- Take off the first letter. Put a new letter at the front so that your word means something you cook in. What letter did you use? (*p*) What word did you make? (*pot*)
- Rearrange the letters to make a word that describes a spinning toy. How did you rearrange the letters? What word did you make? (*top*)
- Take out the vowel. Put a new vowel in to make a word that means to touch lightly. What letter did you use? (*a*) What word did you make? (*tap*)
- Take off the beginning letter. Add a letter that makes a word telling what you use when you travel. What letter did you use? (*m*) What word did you make? (*map*)
- Take out the vowel. Add a different vowel to make a word that describes something you clean the floor with. What letter did you use? (*o*) What word did you make? (*mop*)

Hop, Bunny, Hop *(cont.)*

Change a Word *(cont.)*

- We are going to end with a word that was in the poem. Take off the beginning letter. Put a new letter in its place to make a word that describes what the bunny did. What letter did you use? (*h*) What word did you make? (*hop*)
- What did you notice about the word we started with and the word we ended with?

Closed Word Sort

1. Distribute sets of the *Hop, Bunny, Hop Closed Word Sort* cards (page 12) to individual students, pairs of students, or groups of students.
2. Ask students to put words into groups according to their vowel sounds.
3. Follow the sorting by reading the words and discussing the vowel sounds.
4. Relate the words to the rhyme (e.g., short /ŏ/ as in *hop*; short /ŭ/ as in *bunny*).

Rhyming Riddles

1. Ask students to think of as many words with the short /ŭ/ sound as possible. Have them share their words with partners.
2. Record their words on the board.
3. Distribute *Hop, Bunny, Hop Rhyming Riddles* (page 13) to students and make connections between the words students come up with in Step 1 with the words in the Word Bank.
4. Instruct students to use words from the Word Bank to complete the riddles. Tell them that they will not use one of the words.
5. Have students illustrate one of the rhyming riddles on the backs of their papers.

Writing Connection 

1. Have students write lists of foods a bunny would like to eat. Encourage developmental spelling.
2. Have students share their lists with partners.

Reader's Theater

1. Distribute the *Hop, Bunny, Hop Reader's Theater* script (page 14) to students.
2. Assign parts for eight readers.
3. Have students mark their parts according to the script.
4. Allow several rehearsals to develop fluency.
5. Perform the reader's theater for the class, another class, or for a special school event.

Hop, Bunny, Hop

by Karen McGuigan Brothers

Hop, bunny, hop.
Hop, bunny, hop.
Stopping in the garden
To eat a carrot top.

Run, bunny, run,
Do not stop!
Farmer Brown is coming
To chase you with a mop!

Rest, bunny, rest,
Safe and sound,
Sleeping in your burrow
So deep under the ground.

Hop, Bunny, Hop

Closed Word Sort

Directions: Cut apart the cards. Then, sort them into groups that have the same vowel sound.

hop	not
mop	pot
hot	bunny
run	funny
top	stop
sun	bun

Name: ____________________

Hop, Bunny, Hop

Rhyming Riddles

Directions: Use words from the Word Bank to complete the riddles about bunnies. **Note:** You will not use one of the words.

Word Bank

sun	run	bus	mud	tub	fun

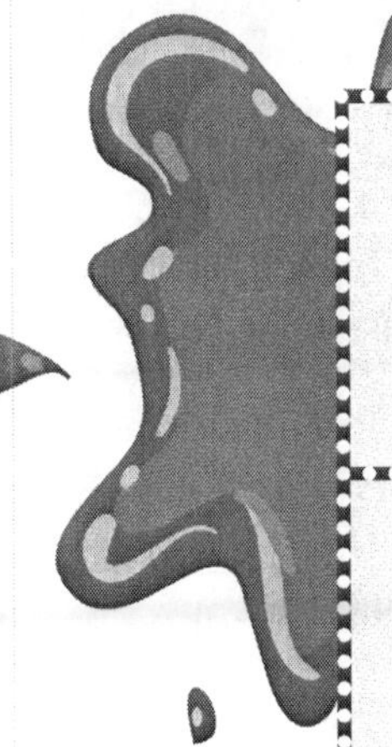

1. a bunny getting a tan

   a bunny in the ____________________

2. a bunny taking a bath

   a bunny in the ____________________

3. a bunny getting dirty

   a bunny in the ____________________

4. a bunny that goes fast

   a bunny that can ____________________

5. a bunny playing with friends

   a bunny having ____________________

Hop, Bunny, Hop

Reader's Theater

All: Hop, Bunny, Hop

All: Hop, bunny, hop.
Hop, bunny, hop.

Reader 1: Stopping in the garden

Reader 2: To eat a carrot top.

All: Run, bunny, run,

Reader 3: do not stop!

Reader 4: Farmer Brown is coming

Reader 5: to chase you with a mop!

All: Rest, bunny, rest,

Reader 6: Safe and sound,

Reader 7: Sleeping in your burrow

Reader 8: So deep under the ground.

Hey Diddle Diddle

Standards

- Describe characters, setting, and major events in a story, using key details.
- Know the spelling-sound correspondences for common consonant digraphs.
- Use end punctuation for sentences.
- Spell untaught words phonetically, drawing on phonemic awareness and spelling conventions.
- See Appendix C for additional standards.

Materials

- *Hey Diddle Diddle* (page 17)
- *Letter Cards* (page 134)
- *Hey Diddle Diddle Open Word Sort* (page 18)
- *Hey Diddle Diddle Rhyming Riddles* (page 19)
- *Hey Diddle Diddle Reader's Theater* (pages 20–23)

Procedures

Introducing the Rhyme

1. Distribute the *Hey Diddle Diddle* rhyme (page 17) to students.
2. Divide the class into five groups.
3. Since this is one of the more common nursery rhymes, all or most of your students may be able to recite it without the text. In order to encourage students to track print, divide the class and ask them to mark their parts.

   All: Hey Diddle Diddle (title)

   Group 1: Hey diddle diddle

   Group 2: The cat and the fiddle,

   Group 3: The cow jumped over the moon.

   Group 4: The little dog laughed

   Group 5: To see such sport

   All: And the dish ran away with the spoon.

4. Read the rhyme several times to develop fluency and to practice reading it as if one voice were reading the entire rhyme.
5. Allow students to illustrate the rhyme and add it to their individual poetry notebooks.
6. Have students add the title to their notebooks' tables of contents.

Change a Word

1. Distribute a set of *Letter Cards* (page 134) to each student. If this activity is used early in the year, we recommend you use only the letters they will need (*d, i, s, h, a, t, o, o, p, l, y, e, g, n*).
2. Before you begin to play Change a Word, have students identify the letters and corresponding sounds.
3. Allow students time to arrange the letters to make their own words.
4. After students have had time to make and share words, ask them to put the letters in a pile and follow your instructions. Tell students each new word will be made by using the last letter of the previous word (*dish-hat-top-played-dogs-spoon*). Say the following:
   - We are going to begin by making a word that is in the rhyme *Hey Diddle Diddle.* We will start with the word *dish.* Then, each new word we make will begin with the last letter of the word before it. Use four letters to make the word *dish.* What letters did you use? Let's say the word and stretch it out.

Hey Diddle Diddle *(cont.)*

Change a Word *(cont.)*

- Put the last letter aside and remove the others. What letter did you save? (*h*) Add two letters so that your word means something the dog could wear on his head when he laughs. What letters did you use? (*a*, *t*) What word did you make? (*hat*)
- Put the last letter aside and remove the others. What letter did you save? (*t*) Add two letters to tell what part of the moon the cow would have jumped over; she would have to jump over the ______. What letters did you use? (*o*, *p*) What word did you make? (*top*)
- Put the last letter aside and remove the others. What letter did you save? (*p*) Add some letters to make the word that tells what the cat did with the fiddle. What letters did you add? (*l*, *a*, *y*, *e*, *d*). What word did you make? (*played*)
- Put the last letter aside and remove the others. What letter did you save? (*d*) Add some letters to make the word that means more than one dog. What letters did you use? (*o*, *g*, *s*) What word did you make? (*dogs*)
- Put the last letter aside and remove the others. What letter did you save? (*s*) We are going to end with a word that was in the poem. Add some letters to make the word that tells what the dish ran away with. What letters did you use? (*p*, *o*, *o*, *n*). What word did you make? (*spoon*)
- What did you notice about the word we started with and the word we ended with?

Open Word Sort

1. Distribute sets of the *Hey Diddle Diddle Open Word Sort* cards (page 18) to individual students, pairs of students, or groups of students.
2. Have students read the words and decide how they can be sorted. Most students will sort the words into groups based on rhyme. However, other sorts should be accepted as long as students can explain what the words have in common.
3. Follow the sorting with a discussion of word meanings and different ways groups were created.

Rhyming Riddles

1. Ask students to think of as many words with the *-ow* ending as they can. Have them share their words with partners.
2. Record their words on the board.
3. Distribute *Hey Diddle Diddle Rhyming Riddles* (page 19) to students.
4. Instruct students to use words from the Word Bank to complete the riddles. Tell them that they will not use one of the words.
5. Have students illustrate one of the rhyming riddles on the backs of their papers.

Writing Connection

1. Have students write sentences describing what the moon might say to the cow.
2. Have students share their sentences with the class.

Reader's Theater

1. Distribute the *Hey Diddle Diddle Reader's Theater* script (pages 20–23) to students.
2. Assign parts for five readers.
3. Have students mark their parts according to the script.
4. Allow several rehearsals to develop fluency.
5. Perform the reader's theater for the class, another class, or for a special school event.

Hey Diddle Diddle

Traditional Rhyme

Hey diddle diddle,

The cat and the fiddle,

The cow jumped over the moon.

The little dog laughed

To see such sport,

And the dish ran away with
the spoon.

Hey Diddle Diddle

Open Word Sort

Directions: Cut apart the cards. Then, sort them into groups that you choose. Be ready to explain your groups.

spoon	middle
diddle	riddle
wish	fish
dish	noon
codfish	balloon
cartoon	raccoon
soon	fiddle

Name: ______________________________

Hey Diddle Diddle

Rhyming Riddles

Directions: Use words from the Word Bank to complete the riddles about cows. **Note:** You will not use one of the words.

Word Bank

sow	vow	meow	bow	chow	wow

1. what the cow does at the end of a play

   The cow takes a ______________.

2. a cow that thinks she's a cat

   a cow that says ______________

3. a cow that thinks she's a female pig

   a cow that thinks she's a ______________

4. a cow that is excited at what she sees

   a cow that says ______________

5. a cow that likes to eat

   a cow that likes to ______________ down

Hey Diddle Diddle

Reader's Theater

All: Hey Diddle Diddle

Reader 1: Here's an interesting rhyme:

Hey diddle diddle,
The cat and the fiddle,
The cow jumped over the moon.

Reader 2: A cow can't jump over the moon.

Reader 3: Maybe it just means that the cow jumped really high.

Reader 4: I never saw a cow jump.

Reader 5: Maybe something scared her.

Reader 2: It was probably that cat playing a fiddle.

Reader 3: It didn't say the cat was playing the fiddle. Maybe the cat was just sitting by the fiddle.

Reader 4: I think the cat was playing a little cat-sized fiddle. That would make me jump.

Reader 5: Is that the end of the rhyme?

Hey Diddle Diddle

Reader's Theater *(cont.)*

Reader 1: No. There's more:

Hey diddle diddle,
The cat and the fiddle,
The cow jumped over the moon.
The little dog laughed
To see such sport.

Reader 2: I never heard a dog laugh.

Reader 3: We had a dog that could smile.

Reader 4: Really?

Reader 3: If he was happy to see me, he would smile.

Reader 2: Did he ever laugh?

Reader 3: No. He never laughed.

Reader 2: Well the dog in this rhyme laughed.

Reader 3: Maybe he was just really smart.

Reader 5: Is that the end of the rhyme?

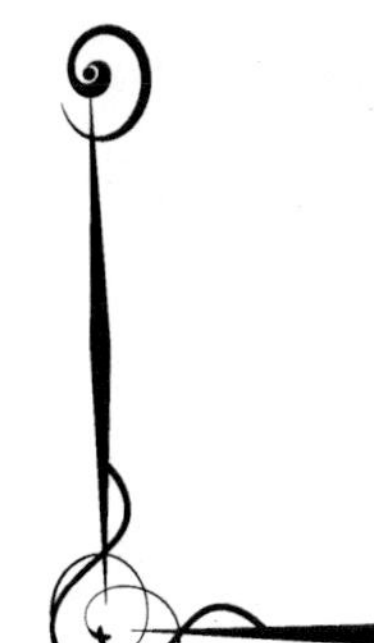

Hey Diddle Diddle

Reader's Theater *(cont.)*

Reader 1: No. Here's the rest:

Hey diddle diddle,
The cat and the fiddle,
The cow jumped over the moon.
The little dog laughed
To see such sport,
And the dish ran away with the spoon.

Reader 2: Dishes and spoons can't run.

Reader 3: Maybe something else happened.

Reader 2: What?

Reader 4: Maybe someone threw the dish and spoon away and told their mom it ran away.

Reader 5: I think I know what really happened.

Reader 4: What?

Reader 5: I think this is a story made up by a really bad child. First, he pulled the cat's tail and it screeched. When his mother heard it and asked what happened, he said that the cat jumped across the fiddle and made the sound.

Reader 4: Then what?

Hey Diddle Diddle

Reader's Theater *(cont.)*

Reader 5: Then, the child left the gate open and the cow got out and ran into the field. When his mother asked what the cow was doing in the field, the child said the cow got scared when the cat ran across the fiddle, and jumped so high that it landed in the field.

Reader 3: What about the laughing dog?

Reader 5: There was no laughing dog. The child himself laughed when he thought his mother believed those stories. The mother heard him, asked what he was laughing about, and the child blamed the laughing on the dog.

Reader 2: What about the dish and spoon?

Reader 5: I think that the mother knew the child was lying to her, so she sent him to bed without any supper. When he asked why, she said, "Because your dish ran away with your spoon."

Reader 4: And that showed him how silly his lies were.

Reader 5: Right. And it also taught him another lesson.

Reader 1: What lesson?

Reader 5: If you lie to your mother, you will get caught.

Fuzzy Wuzzy

Standards

- Demonstrate understanding of spoken words, syllables, and sounds.
- Use conventional spelling for words with common spelling patterns and for frequently occurring irregular words.
- Spell untaught words phonetically, drawing on phonemic awareness and spelling conventions.
- Write narratives in which they recount a well-elaborated event or short sequence of events. Include details to describe actions, thoughts, and feelings, use temporal words to signal event order, and provide a sense of closure.
- See Appendix C for additional standards.

Materials

- *Fuzzy Wuzzy* (page 26)
- *Fuzzy Wuzzy Word Ladder* (page 27)
- *Fuzzy Wuzzy Open Word Sort* (page 28)
- *Fuzzy Wuzzy Rhyming Riddles* (page 29)
- *Fuzzy Wuzzy Reader's Theater* (pages 30–31)

Procedures

Introducing the Rhyme

1. Recite the rhyme to students. Tell students to close their eyes and make a mental image of the rhyme as you read it to them.
2. Have students open their eyes and share their images with partners.
3. Distribute the *Fuzzy Wuzzy* rhyme (page 26) to students.
4. Read the rhyme chorally several times to develop fluency.
5. Allow students to illustrate the rhyme and add it to their individual poetry notebooks.
6. Have students add the title to their notebooks' tables of contents.

Word Ladder

1. Distribute *Fuzzy Wuzzy Word Ladder* (page 27) to students.
2. Allow students time to observe the illustrations on their activity sheets.
3. After students have had time to review their activity sheets, tell them to follow your clues to make a word ladder from *bear* to *hair*. Say the following:
    - start at the bottom of the ladder—the animal in the rhyme (*bear*)
    - remove one vowel—a chocolate candy ______ (*bar*)
    - change one letter—a vehicle (*car*)
    - change the beginning sound—something in the night sky (*star*)
    - add one vowel—a step (*stair*)
    - change the beginning sound—what Fuzzy Wuzzy didn't have (*hair*)
4. Help students make a meaningful connection between the poem and the first and last rungs of the ladder.

Fuzzy Wuzzy *(cont.)*

Open Word Sort

1. Distribute sets of the *Fuzzy Wuzzy Open Word Sort* cards (page 28) to individual students, pairs of students, or groups of students.
2. Have students read the words and decide how they can be sorted.
3. Follow the sorting with a discussion of word meanings and different ways groups were created.

Rhyming Riddles

1. Ask students to think of as many words that rhyme with the word *bear* as they can. Have them share their words with partners.
2. Record their words on the board.
3. Distribute *Fuzzy Wuzzy Rhyming Riddles* (page 29) to students and make connections between the words students come up with in Step 1 with the words in the Word Bank.
4. Instruct students to use words from the Word Bank to complete the riddles. Tell them that they will not use one of the words.
5. Have students illustrate one of the rhyming riddles on the backs of their papers.

Writing Connection 

1. Have students write sentences describing what they think happened to Fuzzy Wuzzy's hair.
2. Have students share their sentences with partners.

Reader's Theater 

1. Distribute the *Fuzzy Wuzzy Reader's Theater* script (pages 30–31) to students.
2. Allow students to read the script independently.
3. Discuss the script as a class.
4. Assign parts for six readers.
5. Allow several rehearsals to develop fluency.
6. Perform the reader's theater for the class, another class, or for a special school event.

Fuzzy Wuzzy

Traditional Rhyme

Fuzzy Wuzzy was a bear,
Fuzzy Wuzzy had no hair.
Fuzzy Wuzzy wasn't fuzzy,
Was he?

Name: ______________________________

Fuzzy Wuzzy

Word Ladder

Directions: Listen to the clues. Then, write the words on the rungs below as you climb the ladder.

6. hair

5.

4.

3.

2.

1. bear

Fuzzy Wuzzy

Open Word Sort

Directions: Cut apart the cards. Then, sort them into groups that you choose. Be ready to explain your groups.

Fuzzy	Wuzzy
bear	was
wig	hair
fur	fizzy
dizzy	busy
care	bare
bald	he

Name: ____________________

Fuzzy Wuzzy

Rhyming Riddles

Directions: Use words from the Word Bank to complete the riddles about bears. **Note:** You will not use one of the words.

Word Bank

pair	stairs	tear	chairs	hair	bare

1. bears that come in twos
   ____
   bears in a ____________________

2. bears that like going upstairs

   ____
   bears that take ____________________

3. bears that are sitting
   ____
   bears on ____________________

4. bears that rip things
   ____
   bears that ____________________

5. bears that are bald
   ____
   bears with no ____________________

Fuzzy Wuzzy

Reader's Theater

All: Fuzzy Wuzzy

Reader 1: Fuzzy Wuzzy was a bear,

Reader 2: What kind of bear was he?

Reader 3: Was he a teddy bear?

Reader 1: I don't know. Let me finish the rhyme.

Fuzzy Wuzzy was a bear,
Fuzzy Wuzzy had no hair.

Reader 4: What happened to his hair?

Reader 5: Did his hair fall out?

Reader 6: Was he born without hair?

Reader 1: I'm not sure. I'll read the rest:

Fuzzy Wuzzy was a bear,
Fuzzy Wuzzy had no hair.
Fuzzy Wuzzy wasn't fuzzy,
Was he?

Fuzzy Wuzzy

Reader's Theater *(cont.)*

Reader 2: Is that all it says?

Reader 4: What about how he lost his hair?

Reader 3: Poor bear.

Reader 6: Let's change the rhyme.

Reader 1: What do you mean?

Reader 6: Here's what I mean:

Fuzzy Wuzzy was a bear,
Fuzzy Wuzzy grew some hair.
Now he doesn't look so bare,
Does he?

All: Hooray for
Fuzzy Wuzzy!

Pretty Star

Standards

- Know and apply grade-level phonics and word analysis skills in decoding words.
- Use knowledge that every syllable must have a vowel sound to determine the number of syllables in a printed word.
- See Appendix C for additional standards.

Materials

- *Pretty Star* (page 34)
- *Pretty Star Word Ladder* (page 35)
- *Pretty Star Open Word Sort* (page 36)
- *Pretty Star Rhyming Riddles* (page 37)
- *Pretty Star Reader's Theater* (page 38)

Procedures

Introducing the Rhyme

1. Distribute the *Pretty Star* rhyme (page 34) to students.
2. Ask students to follow along as you read the rhyme orally.
3. Read the rhyme chorally several times to develop fluency.
4. Allow students to illustrate the rhyme and add it to their individual poetry notebooks.
5. Have students add the title to their notebooks' tables of contents.

Word Ladder

1. Distribute *Pretty Star Word Ladder* (page 35) to students.
2. Allow students time to observe the illustrations on their activity sheets.
3. After students have had time to review their activity sheets, tell them to follow your clues to make a word ladder from *star* to *sun*. Say the following:
    - start at the bottom of the ladder—There are millions of these in the sky—singular. (*star*)
    - remove one letter—a sticky goo on the road (*tar*)
    - change the last letter—what you get when you are out in the sun (*tan*)
    - change one consonant—This will keep you cool on a hot day. (*fan*)
    - change the vowel—You have ______ when you play with your friends. (*fun*)
    - change the beginning consonant—the largest star (*sun*)
4. Help students make a meaningful connection between the poem and the first and last rungs of the ladder.

Pretty Star *(cont.)*

Open Word Sort 

1. Distribute sets of the *Pretty Star Open Word Sort* cards (page 36) to individual students, pairs of students, or groups of students.
2. Have students read the words and decide how they can be sorted.
3. Follow the sorting with a discussion of word meanings and different ways groups were created.

Rhyming Riddles 

1. Ask students to think of as many words that rhyme with the word *star* as they can. Have them share their words with partners.
2. Record their words on the board.
3. Distribute *Pretty Star Rhyming Riddles* (page 37) to students and make connections between words students come up with in Step 1 with the words in the Word Bank.
4. Instruct students to use words from the Word Bank to complete the riddles. Tell them that they will not use one of the words.
5. Have students illustrate one of the rhyming riddles on the backs of their papers.

Writing Connection 

1. Display the poem for students to see.
2. Randomly point to words in the poem and ask students to clap the number of parts they hear (e.g., *pretty*—2 claps; *up*—one clap).
3. Introduce or review the term *syllables* with the class.
4. Count and record the total number of syllables in each line of the first stanza such as the following:

   3 syllables

   4 syllables

   3 syllables

   4 syllables

5. Have students write their own rhymes following the pattern they discovered. For example:

   Funny clown

   You make me smile.

   I like you,

   Stay awhile.

Reader's Theater 

1. Distribute the *Pretty Star Reader's Theater* script (page 38) to students.
2. Allow students to read the script independently.
3. Discuss the script as a class.
4. Assign parts for four groups.
5. Allow several rehearsals to develop fluency.
6. Perform the reader's theater for the class, another class, or for a special school event.

Pretty Star

by Karen McGuigan Brothers

Pretty star
up in the sky,
how did you
get up so high?

You shine bright
all through the night
until the sun
puts out your light.

Name: ______________________________

Pretty Star

Word Ladder

Directions: Listen to the clues. Then, write the words on the rungs below as you climb the ladder.

6. sun

5.

4.

3.

Sunscreen
SPF 30

2.

1. star

Pretty Star

Open Word Sort

Directions: Cut apart the cards. Then, sort them into groups that you choose. Be ready to explain your groups.

sky	sun
light	up
night	high
bright	shine
star	

Name: ______________________________

Pretty Star

Rhyming Riddles

Directions: Use words from the Word Bank to complete the riddles about stars. **Note:** You will not use one of the words.

Word Bank

far	bar	scar	tar	car	jar

1. a star that eats sweets ______________

a star with a candy ______________

2. a star that walks ten miles ______________

a star that goes ______________

3. a star that drives ______________

a star in a ______________

4. a star with a lid ______________

a star in a ______________

5. a star who once had a bad cut ______________

a star with a ______________

Pretty Star

Reader's Theater

All: Pretty Star

Group 1: Pretty star
up in the sky,

Group 2: How did you
get up so high?

Group 3: You shine bright
all through the night

Group 4: Until the sun
puts out your light.

Peter, Peter, Pumpkin Eater

Standards

- Decode two-syllable words following basic patterns by breaking the words into syllables.
- Know final -*e* and common vowel team conventions for representing long vowel sounds.
- Use end punctuation for sentences.
- Use conventional spelling for words with common spelling patterns and for frequently occurring irregular words.
- Spell untaught words phonetically, drawing on phonemic awareness and spelling conventions.
- See Appendix C for additional standards.

Materials

- *Peter, Peter, Pumpkin Eater* (page 41)
- *Peter, Peter, Pumpkin Eater Word Ladder* (page 42)
- *Peter, Peter, Pumpkin Eater Closed Word Sort* (pages 43–44)
- *Peter, Peter, Pumpkin Eater Rhyming Riddles* (page 45)
- *Peter, Peter, Pumpkin Eater Reader's Theater* (pages 46–47)

Procedures

Introducing the Rhyme

1. Distribute the *Peter, Peter, Pumpkin Eater* rhyme (page 41) to students.
2. Ask students to follow along as you read the rhyme orally.
3. Discuss what is happening in each stanza.
4. Have students use their fingers as pointers to track print as the class reads the rhyme chorally several times to develop fluency.
5. Allow students to illustrate the rhyme and add it to their individual poetry notebooks.
6. Have students add the title to their notebooks' tables of contents.

Word Ladder

1. Distribute *Peter, Peter, Pumpkin Eater Word Ladder* (page 42) to students.
2. Allow students time to observe the illustrations on their activity sheets.
3. After students have had time to review their activity sheets, tell them to follow your clues to make a word ladder from *Peter* to *Peter*. Say the following:
    - start at the bottom of the ladder—the name of the man in the rhyme (*Peter*)
    - change a letter—where we put money to park the car (*meter*)
    - remove two letters—Someone you didn't know before is someone you just ______. (*met*)
    - change a letter—This describes water. (*wet*)
    - change a letter—an animal that lives in your house (*pet*)
    - add two letters—the name of the man in the rhyme (*Peter*)
4. Help students make a meaningful connection between the poem and the first and last rungs of the ladder.

Peter, Peter, Pumpkin Eater *(cont.)*

Closed Word Sort

1. Distribute sets of the *Peter, Peter, Pumpkin Eater Closed Word Sort* cards (pages 43–44) to individual students, pairs of students, or groups of students.
2. Introduce or review the term *syllables* with the class.
3. Ask students to put words into groups according to the number of syllables.
4. Follow the sorting by reading the words and discussing the syllables.
5. Relate the words to the rhyme.

Rhyming Riddles

1. Ask students to think of as many words that rhyme with the word *keep* as they can. Have them share their words with partners.
2. Record their words on the board.
3. Distribute *Peter, Peter, Pumpkin Eater Rhyming Riddles* (page 45) to students and make connections between the words students come up with in Step 1 with the words in the Word Bank.
4. Instruct students to use words from the Word Bank to complete the riddles. Tell them that they will not use one of the words.
5. Have students illustrate one of the rhyming riddles on the backs of their papers.

Writing Connection 

1. Have students think about how Peter's wife feels about being in a pumpkin shell. Have students write what she might say to Peter.
2. Have students share their writing with the class.

Reader's Theater 

1. Distribute the *Peter, Peter, Pumpkin Eater Reader's Theater* script (pages 46–47) to students.
2. Assign parts for five readers.
3. Allow several rehearsals to develop fluency.
4. Perform the reader's theater for the class, another class, or for a special school event.

Peter, Peter, Pumpkin Eater

Traditional Rhyme

Peter, Peter, pumpkin
eater,

Had a wife and
couldn't keep her.

He put her in a
pumpkin shell,

And there he kept her
very well.

Name: ______________________________

Peter, Peter, Pumpkin Eater

Word Ladder

Directions: Listen to the clues. Then, write the words on the rungs below as you climb the ladder.

6. Peter

5.

4.

3.

2.

1. Peter

Peter, Peter, Pumpkin Eater

Closed Word Sort

Directions: Cut apart the cards. Then, sort them into groups that have the same number of syllables.

Peter	pumpkin
put	in
shell	October
pie	wife
eater	Pete
keep	her

Peter, Peter, Pumpkin Eater

Closed Word Sort *(cont.)*

kept	eat
very	well
orange	Halloween
husband	

Name: ______________________________

Peter, Peter, Pumpkin Eater

Rhyming Riddles

Directions: Use words from the Word Bank to complete the riddles about Peter. **Note:** You will not use one of the words.

Word Bank

deep	beep	sheep	peep	sleep	jeep

1. Peter goes for a ride.

Peter is in a ______________.

2. Peter takes some animals for a ride.

The ______________ ride with Peter.

3. Peter's animals don't make a sound.

Peter's animals don't make a ______________.

4. Peter blows the horn.

Peter's horn goes ______________.

5. Peter has to go to bed.

Peter needs to ______________.

Peter, Peter, Pumpkin Eater

Reader's Theater

All: Peter, Peter, Pumpkin Eater

Reader 1: Let's read about
Peter, Peter, pumpkin eater.

Peter, Peter, pumpkin eater,

Reader 2: Did he like pumpkin in a pie?

Reader 3: I like pumpkin pie.

Reader 1: He may have liked it in a pie. It does not say if that's how he liked it.

Reader 4: Maybe he cut the pumpkin open and ate the insides with a spoon.

Reader 5: Yuck! That would make me sick.

Reader 2: A pumpkin is full of seeds and goo.

Reader 1: Let's read some more of the rhyme.

Peter, Peter, pumpkin eater,
Had a wife and couldn't keep her.

Peter, Peter, Pumpkin Eater

Reader's Theater *(cont.)*

Reader 2: Why couldn't he keep her? Didn't she like him anymore?

Reader 3: Maybe he had pumpkin breath.

Reader 1: Let's read on.

Peter, Peter, pumpkin eater,
Had a wife and couldn't keep her.
He put her in a pumpkin shell,
And there he kept her very well.

Reader 4: That must have been a really big pumpkin.

All: Or a very small wife.

There Was an Old Woman Who Lived in a Shoe

Standards

- Identify words and phrases in stories or poems that suggest feelings or appeal to the senses.
- Decode regularly spelled one-syllable words.
- Produce and expand complete simple and compound declarative, interrogative, imperative, and exclamatory sentences in response to prompts.
- Use end punctuation for sentences.
- See Appendix C for additional standards.

Materials

- *There Was an Old Woman Who Lived in a Shoe* (page 50)
- *There Was an Old Woman Who Lived in a Shoe Word Ladder* (page 51)
- *There Was an Old Woman Who Lived in a Shoe Closed Word Sort* (pages 52–53)
- *There Was an Old Woman Who Lived in a Shoe Rhyming Riddles* (page 54)
- *There Was an Old Woman Who Lived in a Shoe Reader's Theater* (pages 55–56)
- index cards

Procedures

Introducing the Rhyme

1. Distribute the *There Was an Old Woman Who Lived in a Shoe* rhyme (page 50) to students.
2. Read the rhyme chorally.
3. Discuss the rhyme. Ask students the following questions:
    - How was the old woman feeling? How do you know?
    - How do you think the children felt? Why do you think so?
4. Write each word of the rhyme on an index card and distribute to students.
5. Have students arrange themselves so that the rhyme is in order.
6. Have students stand in a circle and read the rhyme, with each student reading his or her own card. Encourage them to read the rhyme smoothly so that it seems as if one voice were reading the rhyme.
7. Allow students to illustrate the rhyme and add it to their individual poetry notebooks.
8. Have students add the title to their notebooks' tables of contents.

Word Ladder

1. Distribute *There Was an Old Woman Who Lived in a Shoe Word Ladder* (page 51) to students.
2. Allow students time to observe the illustrations on their activity sheets.
3. After students have had time to review their activity sheets, tell them to follow your clues to make a word ladder from *children* to *bed*. Say the following:
    - start at the bottom of the ladder—many young people (*children*)
    - remove three letters—one young person (*child*)
    - change the last letter—You feel this when a cool breeze blows by. (*chill*)
    - change the beginning sound—another name for a duck's beak (*bill*)
    - change the vowel—This rings when it is time for school to start. (*bell*)
    - change the ending sound—where the Old Woman put the children after she scolded them (*bed*)
4. Help students make a meaningful connection between the poem and the first and last rungs of the ladder.

There Was an Old Woman Who Lived in a Shoe *(cont.)*

Closed Word Sort

1. Distribute sets of the *There Was an Old Woman Who Lived in a Shoe Closed Word Sort* cards (pages 52–53) to individual students, pairs of students, or groups of students.
2. Review with students what singular and plural nouns are.
3. Ask students to put words into groups: singular nouns and plural nouns.
4. Follow the sorting by matching singular and plural noun pairs.
5. Relate the words to the rhyme.

Rhyming Riddles

1. Ask students to think of as many words that rhyme with the word *bed* as they can. Have them share their words with partners.
2. Record their words on the board.
3. Distribute *There Was an Old Woman Who Lived in a Shoe Rhyming Riddles* (page 54) to students and make connections between the words students come up with in Step 1 with the words in the Word Bank.
4. Instruct students to use words from the Word Bank to complete the riddles. Tell them that they will not use one of the words.
5. Have students illustrate one of the rhyming riddles on the backs of their papers.

Writing Connection

1. Have students write a dialogue of what the old woman said when she scolded her children. Encourage them to have the old woman ask questions, use exclamations, make demands, and make statements to her children.
2. Have students share their writing orally with partners or with the class. Remind students to read with expression that fits the characters.

Reader's Theater 

1. Distribute the *There Was an Old Woman Who Lived in a Shoe Reader's Theater* script (pages 55–56) to students.
2. Have students read the script independently.
3. Discuss the script as a class.
4. Assign parts for five readers.
5. Allow several rehearsals to develop fluency.
6. Perform the reader's theater for the class, another class, or for a special school event.

There Was an Old Woman Who Lived in a Shoe

Traditional Rhyme

There was an old woman who
lived in a shoe,

She had so many children she
didn't know what to do;

She gave them some broth
without any bread;

And scolded them
soundly and put them
to bed.

Name: ____________________

There Was an Old Woman Who Lived in a Shoe

Word Ladder

Directions: Listen to the clues. Then, write the words on the rungs below as you climb the ladder.

6. bed

5.

4.

3.

2.

1. children

There Was an Old Woman Who Lived in a Shoe

Closed Word Sort

Directions: Cut apart the cards. Then, sort them into groups: singular nouns and plural nouns.

woman	beds
child	mice
shoe	teeth
bed	men
mouse	boys
tooth	girls

There Was an Old Woman Who Lived in a Shoe

Closed Word Sort *(cont.)*

man	geese
boy	women
girl	children
goose	shoes

Name: ______________________________

There Was an Old Woman Who Lived in a Shoe

Rhyming Riddles

Directions: Use words from the Word Bank to complete the riddles about children. **Note:** You will not use one of the words.

Word Bank

bed	shed	red	sled	fed	sped

1. children who are sleepy

   children in ______________

2. children going down a snowy hill

   children on a ______________

3. children who just ate lunch

   children who were ______________

4. children with sunburns

   children who are ______________

5. children who rode their bikes fast

   children who ______________

There Was an Old Woman Who Lived in a Shoe

Reader's Theater

All: There Was an Old Woman
Who Lived in a Shoe

Reader 1: Here's a rhyme
about an old woman
who lived in a strange place.

There was an old woman who
lived in a shoe,

Reader 2: How could anyone live in a shoe?

Reader 3: Maybe it was a house that looked like a shoe.

Reader 4: I'd like to have a house that looked like a shoe.

Reader 5: I think it would be fun to have a house shaped like a boot.

Reader 4: Why a boot?

Reader 5: Because then it would be big enough for an upstairs.

Reader 1: Let me finish reading about the woman in the shoe.

Readers 2–5: Okay.

Reader 1: There was an old woman who lived in a shoe,
She had so many children she didn't know what to do.

There Was an Old Woman Who Lived in a Shoe

Reader's Theater *(cont.)*

Reader 2: Sounds like she needed a pair of shoes to live in.

Reader 3: Or maybe she should live in a big shoebox.

Reader 1: Here's the rest of the rhyme:

There was an old woman who lived in a shoe,
She had so many children she didn't know what to do;
She gave them some broth without any bread;
And scolded them soundly and put them to bed.

Reader 4: That doesn't sound like much of a supper.

Reader 5: Maybe she didn't have much money for food.

Reader 4: She should have fixed macaroni and cheese. That doesn't cost very much.

Reader 5: Or she could have made them a peanut butter and jelly sandwich.

Reader 3: Even a bowl of oatmeal would have been good.

Reader 2: I wonder why she scolded her children and put them to bed?

Reader 3: Maybe they were making too much noise.

Reader 1: Or maybe they were complaining about the bad supper!

Fireflies

Standards

- Demonstrate command of the conventions of standard English grammar and usage when writing or speaking.
- Use adjectives and adverbs, and choose between them depending on what is to be modified.
- Use words and phrases acquired through conversations, reading and being read to, and responding to texts, including using adjectives and adverbs to describe.
- See Appendix C for additional standards.

Materials

- *Fireflies* (page 59)
- *Fireflies Word Ladder* (page 60)
- *Fireflies Closed Word Sort* (page 61)
- *Fireflies Rhyming Riddles* (page 62)
- *Fireflies Reader's Theater* (page 63)
- online pictures or videos of fireflies *(optional)*

Procedures

Introducing the Rhyme

1. Ask students to share their experiences with observing or catching fireflies. If students have not had experiences with fireflies, show pictures or video clips from the Internet.
2. Distribute the *Fireflies* rhyme (page 59) to students.
3. Ask students to follow along as you read the rhyme orally.
4. Read the rhyme chorally several times to develop fluency.
5. Allow students to illustrate the rhyme and add it to their individual poetry notebooks.
6. Have students add the title to their notebooks' tables of contents.

Word Ladder

1. Distribute *Fireflies Word Ladder* (page 60) to students.
2. Allow students time to observe the illustrations on their activity sheets.
3. After students have had time to review their activity sheets, tell them to follow your clues to make a word ladder from *fire* to *flies*. Say the following:
    - start at the bottom of the ladder—It is very hot and starts with a match. (*fire*)
    - change one letter—part of a car (*tire*)
    - remove one letter—Men wear this on their necks. (*tie*)
    - change one letter—a dessert made with fruit (*pie*)
    - add one letter—plural of the last word you made (*pies*)
    - change the beginning sound—what a firefly does (*flies*)
4. Help students make a meaningful connection between the poem and the first and last rungs of the ladder.

Fireflies *(cont.)*

Closed Word Sort 

1. Use the *Fireflies Closed Word Sort* template (page 61) to create word cards from the lists students generated in the *Writing Connection* activity.
2. Distribute sets of word cards to individual students, pairs of students, or groups of students.
3. Review with students what adjectives and adverbs are.
4. Instruct students to sort cards into words that describe fireflies and words that describe how fireflies move.
5. Follow the sorting with a discussion of word meanings.

Rhyming Riddles 

1. Ask students to think of as many words that rhyme with the word *fly* as they can. Have them share their words with partners.
2. Record their words on the board.
3. Distribute *Fireflies Rhyming Riddles* (page 62) to students and make connections between the words students come up with in Step 1 with the words in the Word Bank.
4. Instruct students to use words from the Word Bank to complete the riddles. Tell them that they will not use one of the words.
5. Have students illustrate one of the rhyming riddles on the backs of their papers.

Writing Connection 

1. Divide students into pairs or small groups.
2. Distribute a sheet of writing paper to each group. Model how to fold the paper horizontally to create two columns. **Note:** You may wish to have students use the template on page 61 instead of having them fold paper.
3. Review the terms *adjective* and *adverb* with students.
4. Have students brainstorm and list adjectives that describe fireflies (e.g., *bright, glowing, shiny*) in one column, and adverbs that describe how fireflies move (e.g., *fly, glide, flutter*) in the other column.
5. Collect students' lists and create word cards for the *Fireflies Closed Word Sort* (page 61) activity that correlates with this lesson.

Reader's Theater

1. Distribute the *Fireflies Reader's Theater* script (page 63) to students.
2. Have students read the script independently.
3. Discuss the script as a class.
4. Assign parts for four readers.
5. Allow several rehearsals to develop fluency.
6. Perform the reader's theater for the class, another class, or for a special school event.

Fireflies

by Karen McGuigan Brothers

Lighting up the summer sky,

flying low,

flying high,

flying here,

flying there,

Fireflies are everywhere.

Name: ______________________________

Fireflies

Word Ladder

Directions: Listen to the clues. Then, write the words on the rungs below as you climb the ladder.

Fireflies

Closed Word Sort

Teacher Directions: Write adjectives and adverbs about fireflies on the cards below. Then, cut them apart. Have students sort them into the two groups: adjectives that describe fireflies and adverbs that describe how fireflies move.

Name: ____________________

Fireflies

Rhyming Riddles

Directions: Use words from the Word Bank to complete the riddles about fireflies. **Note:** You will not use one of the words.

Word Bank

sky	dry	cry	bye	shy	buy

1. fireflies that are sad

   fireflies that ____________________

2. fireflies that are up high

   fireflies in the ____________________

3. fireflies that are not wet

   fireflies that are ____________________

4. fireflies that are leaving

   fireflies saying ____________________

5. fireflies that don't talk much

   fireflies that are ____________________

Fireflies

Reader's Theater

All: Fireflies

All: Lighting up the summer sky,

Reader 1: flying low,

Readers 1–2: flying high,

Readers 1–3: flying here,

Reader 1–4: flying there,

All: Fireflies are everywhere.

Rubber Duck

Standards

- Know and apply grade-level phonics and word analysis skills in decoding words.
- Use frequently occurring adjectives.
- Produce complete sentences when appropriate to task and situation.
- Decode regularly spelled one-syllable words.
- See Appendix C for additional standards.

Materials

- *Rubber Duck* (page 66)
- *Rubber Duck Word Ladder* (page 67)
- *Rubber Duck Closed Word Sort* (pages 68–69)
- *Rubber Duck Rhyming Riddles* (page 70)
- *Rubber Duck Reader's Theater* (pages 71–72)

Procedures

Introducing the Rhyme

1. Distribute the *Rubber Duck* rhyme (page 66) to students.
2. Ask students to follow along as you read the rhyme orally.
3. Read the rhyme chorally several times to develop fluency.
4. Allow students to illustrate the rhyme and add it to their individual poetry notebooks.
5. Have students add the title to their notebooks' tables of contents.

Word Ladder

1. Distribute *Rubber Duck Word Ladder* (page 67) to students.
2. Allow students time to observe the illustrations on their activity sheets.
3. After students have had time to review their activity sheets, tell them to follow your clues to make a word ladder from *duck* to *quack*. Say the following:
    - start at the bottom of the ladder—an animal that makes the sound "quack" (*duck*)
    - change one letter—when you have good fortune (*luck*)
    - change the vowel—what you do with a lollipop (*lick*)
    - change the first letter to a blend—You can teach a dog to do this. (*trick*)
    - change the vowel—what a train runs on (*track*)
    - change the beginning sound blend—the sound a duck makes (*quack*)
4. Help students make a meaningful connection between the poem and the first and last rungs of the ladder.

Rubber Duck *(cont.)*

Closed Word Sort 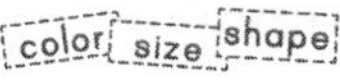

1. Distribute sets of the *Rubber Duck Closed Word Sort* cards (pages 68–69) to individual students, pairs of students, or groups of students.
2. Review what rhyming words are with the class.
3. Ask students to create groups of rhyming words using their cards.
4. Follow the sorting with a discussion of word meanings and the vowel rule.
5. Relate the words to the rhyme.

Rhyming Riddles 

1. Ask students to think of as many words that rhyme with the word *quack* as they can. Have them share their words with partners.
2. Record their words on the board.
3. Distribute *Rubber Duck Rhyming Riddles* (page 70) to students and make connections between the words students come up with in Step 1 with the words in the Word Bank.
4. Instruct students to use words from the Word Bank to complete the riddles. Tell them that they will not use one of the words.
5. Have students illustrate one of the rhyming riddles on the backs of their papers.

Writing Connection 

1. Choose a noun from the poem (e.g., *duck, pool, school*).
2. Pick three categories to describe the noun (e.g., *color, size, actions*).
3. List words under each category.
4. Pick a favorite word from each list and write a new poem.
5. End the poem with a statement or word that sums up the subject.

Example

Dogs (noun)

Brown (color)

Big (size)

Running (action)

Lots of fun!

Reader's Theater 

1. Distribute the *Rubber Duck Reader's Theater* script (pages 71–72) to students.
2. Have students read the script independently.
3. Assign parts for five readers.
4. Allow several rehearsals to develop fluency.
5. Perform the reader's theater for the class, another class, or for a special school event.

Rubber Duck

by Karen McGuigan Brothers

Rubber duck
In my pool
Swims while I
Get dressed for school.

I said I would
Soon be back.
He just swam
And said, "Quack quack."

Name: ______________________________

Rubber Duck

Word Ladder

Directions: Listen to the clues. Then, write the words on the rungs below as you climb the ladder.

6. quack

5.

4.

3.

2.

1. duck

Rubber Duck

Closed Word Sort

Directions: Cut apart the cards. Then, sort them into groups of rhyming words. Be ready to explain your groups.

shoot	hoot
pool	toot
spoon	boom
room	boot
stool	fool
root	raccoon

Rubber Duck

Closed Word Sort (cont.)

noon	broom
tool	cool
school	moon
soon	groom

Name: ______________________________

Rubber Duck

Rhyming Riddles

Directions: Use words from the Word Bank to complete the riddles about ducks. **Note:** You will not use one of the words.

Word Bank

rack	back	snack	pack	quack	black

1. ducks going on a trip

   ducks that have to ______________

2. ducks that are not in the front

   ducks that are in the ______________

3. ducks that like a dark color

   ducks that like ______________

4. ducks that like to eat

   ducks that like to ______________

5. ducks that make noise

   ducks that ______________

Rubber Duck

Reader's Theater

All: Rubber Duck

Reader 1: Rubber duck
In my pool

Reader 2: I used to have a rubber duck.

Reader 3: Was he in your pool?

Reader 2: No, but I took him in the bathtub with me.

Reader 4: Did he swim around?

Reader 2: He swam around when I made waves with my hand.

Reader 1: Well, this rubber duck was in a pool. Let me finish the rhyme.

Reader 2: Okay.

Reader 1: Rubber duck
In my pool
Swims while I
Get dressed for school.

Reader 5: Fish are in a school.

Reader 1: What?

Rubber Duck

Reader's Theater *(cont.)*

Reader 5: Fish travel in a school. You know, a school of fish. I wonder what a group of ducks is called?

Reader 1: Probably a flock, like geese.

Reader 3: I'm pretty sure a group of geese is called a gaggle.

Reader 4: That's a funny word. Gaggle.

Reader 3: Well, that's what a group of geese is called.

Reader 1: I still think a group of ducks is called a flock.

Reader 2: You may be right. Read the rest of the rhyme.

Reader 1: Okay.

I said I would
Soon be back.
He just swam
And said, "quack quack."

Reader 2: My rubber duck didn't quack. He squeaked.

Reader 3: Maybe he was broken.

Reader 4: How would a rubber duck get broken?

Reader 5: Maybe he got stepped on by a gaggle of geese.

Three Little Kittens

Standards

- Identify who is telling the story at various points in a text.
- Use conventional spelling for words with common spelling patterns and for frequently occurring irregular words.
- Spell untaught words phonetically, drawing on phonemic awareness and spelling conventions.
- See Appendix C for additional standards.

Materials

- *Three Little Kittens* (page 75)
- *Three Little Kittens Word Ladder* (page 76)
- *Three Little Kittens Open Word Sort* (page 77)
- *Three Little Kittens Rhyming Riddles* (page 78)
- *Three Little Kittens Reader's Theater* (pages 79–81)

Procedures

Introducing the Rhyme

1. Distribute the *Three Little Kittens* rhyme (page 75) to students.
2. Ask students to read the rhyme independently.
3. Ask for student volunteers to read each stanza.
4. Discuss what is happening in each stanza.
5. Divide the class into four groups, and read the rhyme chorally to develop fluency.
6. Allow students to illustrate the rhyme and add it to their individual poetry notebooks.
7. Have students add the title to their notebooks' tables of contents.

Word Ladder

1. Distribute *Three Little Kittens Word Ladder* (page 76) to students.
2. Allow students time to observe the illustrations on their activity sheets.
3. After students have had time to review their activity sheets, tell them to follow your clues to make a word ladder from *cry* to *pie*. Say the following:
   - start at the bottom of the ladder—what the kittens began to do when they lost their mittens (*cry*)
   - change one letter—to force something apart (*pry*)
   - change the vowel—what you do when you buy something (*pay*)
   - change one letter—tapping someone lightly (*pat*)
   - change the vowel—another name for a peach seed (*pit*)
   - change one letter—what the kittens were not allowed to have (*pie*)
4. Help students make a meaningful connection between the poem and the first and last rungs of the ladder.

Three Little Kittens *(cont.)*

Open Word Sort

1. Distribute sets of the *Three Little Kittens Open Word Sort* cards (page 77) to individual students, pairs of students, or groups of students.
2. Have students read the words and decide how they can be sorted.
3. Follow the sorting with a discussion of word meanings and different ways groups were created.
4. Relate the words to the rhyme.

Rhyming Riddles

1. Ask students to think of as many words that rhyme with the word *cry* as they can. Have them share their words with partners.
2. Record their words on the board.
3. Distribute *Three Little Kittens Rhyming Riddles* (page 78) to students and make connections between the words students come up with in Step 1 with the words in the Word Bank.
4. Instruct students to use words from the Word Bank to complete the riddles. Tell them that they will not use one of the words.
5. Have students illustrate one of the rhyming riddles on the backs of their papers.

Writing Connection 

1. Have students brainstorm lists of places where the kittens might have lost their mittens. Encourage them to use developmental spelling if they need it.
2. Have students share their lists with the class.
3. Count how many different places the class identified.

Reader's Theater 

1. Distribute the *Three Little Kittens Reader's Theater* script (pages 79–81) to students.
2. Assign parts for four readers.
3. Allow several rehearsals to develop fluency.
4. Perform the reader's theater for the class, another class, or for a special school event.

Three Little Kittens

Traditional Rhyme

Three little kittens
Lost their mittens
And they began to cry.
"Oh, mother dear, we sadly fear
Our mittens we have lost."

"What! Lost your mittens,
you silly kittens!
Then you shall have no pie.
Mee-ow, mee-ow, mee-ow.
No, you shall have no pie."

The three little kittens,
They found their mittens,
And they began to cry,
"Oh, mother dear, see here, see here,
Our mittens we have found."

"Put on your mittens,
you happy kittens,
and you shall have some pie."
"Purr-r, purr-r, purr-r,
Oh, let us have some pie."

Name: ______________________________

Three Little Kittens

Word Ladder

Directions: Listen to the clues. Then, write the words on the rungs below as you climb the ladder.

6. pie

5.

4.

3.

2.

1. cry

Three Little Kittens

Open Word Sort

Directions: Cut apart the cards. Then, sort them into groups that you choose. Be ready to explain your groups.

kittens	mee-ow
mittens	cry
mother	lost
pie	purr
cats	gloves
mom	little

Name: ______________________________

Three Little Kittens

Rhyming Riddles

Directions: Use words from the Word Bank to complete the riddles about kittens. **Note:** You will not use one of the words.

Word Bank

try	my	fry	cry	fly	dry

1. kittens who want to do their best

   kittens who ______________

2. kittens who cook bacon

   kittens who ______________

3. kittens who belong to me

   ______________ kittens

4. kittens who go up in a plane

   kittens who ______________

5. kittens who use a towel

   kittens who ______________

Three Little Kittens

Reader's Theater

All: Three Little Kittens

Reader 1: I like this rhyme.
It's about kittens.
I like kittens.

Reader 2: I like kittens, too.
Read the rhyme.

Reader 1: Three little kittens
Lost their mittens
And they began to cry.

Reader 2: Wait a minute. Kittens don't wear mittens. Mittens are for hands and they don't have hands; they have feet. They would have to wear socks and they don't like socks.

Reader 3: How do you know?

Reader 2: My sister put doll socks on our cat once and he hated them. They made him walk funny.

Reader 1: Well, in this rhyme, they wear mittens.
Can I please finish the rhyme?

Reader 2: Go ahead.

Three Little Kittens

Reader's Theater *(cont.)*

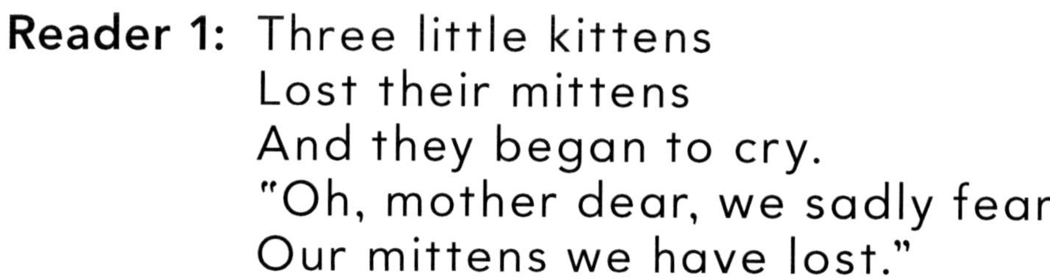

Reader 1: Three little kittens
Lost their mittens
And they began to cry.
"Oh, mother dear, we sadly fear
Our mittens we have lost."

"What?! Lost your mittens,
you silly kittens!
Then you shall have no pie."
Mee-ow, mee-ow, mee-ow.
"No, you shall have no pie."

Reader 3: Cats don't eat pie. Cats eat cat food.

Reader 4: Maybe some cats like pie.

Reader 3: My cat doesn't like pie. When he was a kitten, he liked milk. Now that he's grown, he eats cat food. He eats Crunchy Bits and if my mom buys another brand of cat food, he won't even eat that. From time to time, he's eaten little bits of leftover chicken, but he wouldn't dream of eating any pie.

Reader 1: Well, apparently the cats in this rhyme do like pie or their mother wouldn't have used it as punishment for losing their mittens. I'll finish the rhyme.

Readers 2–4: Okay.

Three Little Kittens

Reader's Theater *(cont.)*

Reader 1: The three little kittens,
They found their mittens,
And they began to cry,
"Oh, mother dear, see here, see here,
Our mittens we have found."

"Put on your mittens,
you happy kittens,
and you shall have some pie.
Purr-r, purr-r, purr-r,
Oh, let us have some pie."

Reader 4: I'm going to write my own rhyme.

Reader 3: What is it about?

Reader 4: Three cats that wear hats.

Reader 2: Do they eat pie?

Reader 4: No. They eat rats.

Readers 1–3: Yuck. That's gross.

Reader 4: The cats don't think so.

Humpty Dumpty

Standards

- Use illustrations and details in a story to describe its characters, setting, or events.
- Use words and phrases acquired through conversations, reading and being read to, and responding to texts.
- Use singular and plural nouns with matching verbs in sentences.
- Write narratives in which they recount a well-eloborated event or short sequence of events. Include details to describe actions, thoughts, and feelings, use temporal words to signal event order, and provide a sense of closure.
- See Appendix C for additional standards.

Materials

- *Humpty Dumpty* (page 84)
- *Humpty Dumpty Word Ladder* (page 85)
- *Humpty Dumpty Closed Word Sort* (pages 86–87)
- *Humpty Dumpty Rhyming Riddles* (page 88)
- *Humpty Dumpty Reader's Theater* (pages 89–91)
- Online illustrations of the rhyme

Procedures

Introducing the Rhyme

1. Distribute the *Humpty Dumpty* rhyme (page 84) to students.
2. Divide the class into nine groups.
3. Since this is one of the more common nursery rhymes, all or most of your students may be able to recite it without the text. In order to encourage students to track print, divide the class and ask them to mark their parts. Then, instruct them to follow the print so that the reading is fluent, as if one voice were reading the entire rhyme.

   Group 1: Humpty

   Group 2: Dumpty

   Group 3: Sat on a wall,

   Group 4: Humpty

   Group 5: Dumpty

   Group 6: Had a great fall.

   Group 7: Not all the king's horses

   Group 8: Nor all the king's men

   Group 9: Could put Humpty Dumpty

   All: Together again.
4. Help students explore various illustrations of the rhyme found online.
5. Discuss how illustrations create different characters or settings.
6. Allow students to illustrate the rhyme and add it to their individual poetry notebooks.
7. Have students add the title to their notebooks' tables of contents.

Word Ladder

1. Distribute *Humpty Dumpty Word Ladder* (page 85) to students.
2. Allow students time to observe the illustrations on their activity sheets.
3. After students have had time to review their activity sheets, tell them to follow your clues to make a word ladder from *wall* to *fall*. Say the following:
   - start at the bottom of the ladder—what Humpty Dumpty sat on (*wall*)
   - change one consonant—A giant is very ______. (*tall*)

Humpty Dumpty *(cont.)*

Word Ladder *(cont.)*

- change one letter—A dog wags this. (*tail*)
- change one letter—another name for letters with stamps (*mail*)
- change one letter—a place to shop (*mall*)
- change one letter—what Humpty Dumpty had (*fall*)

4. Help students make a meaningful connection between the poem and the first and last rungs of the ladder.

Closed Word Sort

1. Distribute sets of the *Humpty Dumpty Closed Word Sort* cards (pages 86–87) to individual students, pairs of students, or groups of students.
2. Review with students what singular and plural nouns are.
3. Ask students to put words into groups: singular nouns and plural nouns.
4. Discuss how verb tenses correspond to singular or plural nouns.
5. Relate the words to the rhyme.

Rhyming Riddles

1. Ask students to think of as many words that rhyme with the word *dump* as they can. Have them share their words with partners.
2. Record their words on the board.
3. Distribute *Humpty Dumpty Rhyming Riddles* (page 88) to students and make connections between the words students come up with in Step 1 with the words in the Word Bank.
4. Instruct students to use words from the Word Bank to complete the riddles. Tell them that they will not use one of the words.
5. Have students illustrate one of the rhyming riddles on the backs of their papers.

Writing Connection 

1. Have students brainstorm what will happen next to Humpty Dumpty. Have them write down their thoughts.
2. Have students share their writing with the class.

Reader's Theater 

1. Distribute the *Humpty Dumpty Reader's Theater* script (pages 89–91) to students.
2. Assign parts for five readers.
3. Allow several rehearsals to develop fluency.
4. Perform the reader's theater for the class, another class, or for a special school event.

Humpty Dumpty

Traditional Rhyme

Humpty Dumpty
Sat on a wall,
Humpty Dumpty
Had a great fall.

Not all the king's horses
Nor all the king's men
Could put Humpty Dumpty
Together again.

Name: ______________________________

Humpty Dumpty

Word Ladder

Directions: Listen to the clues. Then, write the words on the rungs below as you climb the ladder.

6. fall

5.

4.

3.

2.

1. wall

Humpty Dumpty

Closed Word Sort

Directions: Cut apart the cards. Then, sort them into groups: singular nouns and plural nouns.

horses	men
king	man
bricks	castle
egg	wall
walls	three
one	Humpty Dumpty
eggs	kings

Humpty Dumpty

Closed Word Sort *(cont.)*

horse	princess
prince	castles
queen	queens

Name: ______________________________

Humpty Dumpty

Rhyming Riddles

Directions: Use words from the Word Bank to complete the riddles about Humpty Dumpty. **Note:** You will not use one of the words.

Word Bank

bump pump grump dump plump jump

1. Humpty Dumpty is on a trampoline.

   Humpty Dumpty likes to ____________.

2. Humpty Dumpty has a big tummy.

   Humpty Dumpty is ____________.

3. Humpty Dumpty gets water from a well.

   Humpty Dumpty has to ____________.

4. Humpty Dumpty sees a huge trash pile.

   Humpty Dumpty sees a ____________.

5. Humpty Dumpty fell and hurt his head.

   Humpty Dumpty got a ____________.

Humpty Dumpty

Reader's Theater

All: Humpty Dumpty

Reader 1: Here's a funny rhyme:

Humpty Dumpty
Sat on a wall.

Reader 2: That is a funny name for a child.

Reader 1: I don't think Humpty Dumpty is a child.

Reader 3: What is he then?

Reader 4: Somebody told me that he was an egg.

Reader 5: Why was an egg sitting on a wall?

Reader 4: I don't know. Maybe somebody put him there.

Reader 2: Okay. Tell me the rest.

Reader 1: Humpty Dumpty
Sat on a wall,
Humpty Dumpty
Had a great fall.

Reader 4: He should have sat in a cup to keep him from rolling off. Did he get hurt?

Reader 1: I don't know. Let me read to find out.

Readers 2–5: Okay.

Humpty Dumpty

Reader's Theater *(cont.)*

Reader 1: Humpty Dumpty
Sat on a wall,
Humpty Dumpty
Had a great fall.
Not all the king's horses
Nor all the king's men
Could put Humpty Dumpty
Together again.

Reader 2: Tape.

Reader 1: What?

Reader 2: He should have been covered with tape.

Reader 3: Why?

Reader 2: If Humpty Dumpty had been covered with tape before he sat on that wall, he would not have broken into pieces.

Reader 4: Maybe they didn't have any tape.

Reader 5: Well then maybe Humpty Dumpty should have been a hard-boiled egg.

Reader 4: How would that have helped? He still would have cracked apart when he fell.

Humpty Dumpty

Reader's Theater *(cont.)*

Reader 3: Yes, but he wouldn't have broken into so many pieces and he would be a lot easier to clean up.

Reader 4: I never thought about the mess.

Reader 2: He should not have sat on that wall in the first place. I hate a story with a sad ending.

Readers 1, 3, 4, 5: Me, too.

Apples

Standards

- Distinguish long from short vowel sounds in spoken single-syllable words.
- Know the spelling-sound correspondences for common consonant digraphs.
- Know final *-e* and common vowel team conventions for representing long vowel sounds.
- See Appendix C for additional standards.

Materials

- *Apples* (page 94)
- *Letter Cards* (page 134)
- *Apples Closed Word Sort* (pages 95–96)
- *Apples Rhyming Riddles* (page 97)
- *Apples Reader's Theater* (page 98)

Procedures

Introducing the Rhyme

1. Distribute the *Apples* rhyme (page 94) to students.
2. Ask students to read the poem independently.
3. Ask students to follow along as you read the rhyme orally.
4. Discuss what is happening in each stanza.
5. Read the rhyme chorally several times to develop fluency.
6. Allow students to illustrate the rhyme and add it to their individual poetry notebooks.
7. Have students add the title to their notebooks' tables of contents.

Change a Word

1. Distribute a set of *Letter Cards* (page 134) to each student. If this activity is used early in the year, we recommend you use only the letters they will need (*a, p, p, l, e, e, s, w, t, t, r*).
2. Before you begin to play Change a Word, have students identify the letters and corresponding sounds.
3. Allow students time to arrange the letters to make their own words.
4. After students have had time to make and share words, ask them to put the letters in a pile and follow your instructions to make a word chain from *apple* to *treat* (*apple-apples-sweet-tart-taste-eat-treat*). Say the following:
   - We are going to begin by writing the name of the fruit that is in this rhyme. What word did you make? (Write *apple* on the board.)
   - Write the plural of *apple*. What word did you make? (Write *apples* on the board.)
   - Use the last letter of *apples* to make the word for how some apples taste. What word did you make? (Write *sweet* on the board.)
   - Use the last letter of *sweet* to make the word for how other apples might taste. It's another word for *sour*. What word did you make? (Write *tart* on the board.)
   - Use the last letter of *tart* to make the word for taking a bite of an apple. You want to see how it will ______. What word did you make? (Write *taste* on the board.)

Apples (cont.)

Change a Word (cont.)

- Use the last letter of *taste* to make the word for what we like to do with apples. What word did you make? (Write *eat* on the board.)
- Use the last letter of *eat* to make a word that rhymes with *eat* and describes a special snack. What word did you make? (Write *treat* on the board.)

Closed Word Sort

1. Distribute sets of the *Apples Closed Word Sort* cards (pages 95–96) to individual students, pairs of students, or groups of students.
2. Ask students to put words into groups according to their long and short vowel sounds.
3. Relate the words to the rhyme.

Rhyming Riddles

1. Ask students to think of as many words that rhyme with the word *eat* as they can. Have them share their words with partners.
2. Record their words on the board.
3. Distribute *Apples Rhyming Riddles* (page 97) to students and make connections between words students come up with in Step 1 with the words in the Word Bank.
4. Instruct students to use words from the Word Bank to complete the riddles. Tell them that they will not use one of the words.
5. Have students illustrate one of the rhyming riddles on the backs of their papers.

Writing Connection

1. Review with students what an *adjective* is.
2. Have students write lists of adjectives to pair with the word *apples* (e.g., *green apples, yellow apples, yummy apples, big apples, small apples, red delicious apples*).
3. Have students share their lists with the class.
4. Count how many different adjectives the class brainstormed.

Reader's Theater

1. Distribute the *Apples Reader's Theater* script (page 98) to students.
2. Have students read the script independently.
3. Discuss the script.
4. Assign parts for five readers.
5. Allow several rehearsals to develop fluency.
6. Perform the reader's theater for the class, another class, or for a special school event.

Apples

by Karen McGuigan Brothers

So many kinds
of apples to buy;
I like mine baked
inside a pie.

I like it warm
with ice cream on top.
I eat and eat;
It's hard to stop.

I sometimes eat
an apple with lunch.
I like the taste,
I like the crunch.

Or sliced and dipped
In caramel goo.
Apples are good
and good for you.

Apples

Closed Word Sort

Directions: Cut apart the cards. Then, sort them into groups based on long and short vowel sounds.

kinds	so
apples	like
sliced	with
in	it
on	top
stop	lunch
buy	mine

Apples

Closed Word Sort *(cont.)*

pie	I
baked	ice
cream	eat
taste	crunch
dipped	

Name: ______________________________

Apples

Rhyming Riddles

Directions: Use words from the Word Bank to complete the riddles about apples. **Note:** You will not use one of the words.

Word Bank

seat	cheat	treat	neat	heat	eat

1. apples we put in our mouths and chew ____________

apples we ____________

2. apples we warm on the stove ____________

apples we ____________

3. apples that are in a chair ____________

apples in a ____________

4. apples that are a special snack ____________

apples that are a ____________

5. apples that are tidy ____________

apples that are ____________

Apples

Reader's Theater

All: Apples

Reader 1: That poem made me hungry.

Reader 2: Me, too. I wish I had an apple right now.

Reader 3: My mom makes applesauce.

Reader 4: How do you make applesauce?

Reader 3: First, you peel the apples. Then, you cut them up into bite-sized pieces, cover them just to the top with water, and cook them on the stove until they are soft.

Reader 5: Then what?

Reader 3: Then, you take them off the stove and mash the apples until they turn into applesauce.

Reader 5: Do you put anything else in the pan?

Reader 3: My mom always adds some sugar and cinnamon.

Reader 1: Oh! That must smell wonderful.

Reader 3: Yes, it does. I will ask my mother to make some applesauce to bring to school so that everyone can have a taste.

All: Hooray!

The Animal Band

Standards

- Know and apply grade-level phonics and word analysis skills in decoding words.
- Recognize and read grade-appropriate irregularly spelled words.
- Spell untaught words phonetically, drawing on phonemic awareness and spelling conventions.
- See Appendix C for additional standards.

Materials

- *The Animal Band* (page 101)
- *The Animal Band Word Ladder* (page 102)
- *The Animal Band Open Word Sort* (pages 103–104)
- *The Animal Band Rhyming Riddles* (page 105)
- *The Animal Band Reader's Theater* (page 106)

Procedures

Introducing the Rhyme

1. Distribute *The Animal Band* rhyme (page 101) to students.
2. Ask students to read the poem independently.
3. Read the rhyme chorally, encouraging students to make animal sounds at appropriate places in the text.
4. Allow students to illustrate the rhyme and add it to their individual poetry notebooks.
5. Have students add the title to their notebooks' tables of contents.

Word Ladder

1. Distribute *The Animal Band Word Ladder* (page 102) to students.
2. Allow students time to observe the illustrations on their activity sheets.
3. After students have had time to review their activity sheets, tell them to follow your clues to make a word ladder from *band* to *grand*. Say the following:
   - start at the bottom of the ladder—a word in the poem that describes a group that plays music (*band*)
   - remove one letter—A bruise on an apple means it's ______.(*bad*)
   - change the first letter—another word for unhappy (*sad*)
   - add one letter—something found on a beach (*sand*)
   - change one letter—what your fingers are on (*hand*)
   - change the beginning sound—how the band in the poem sounded (*grand*)
4. Help students make a meaningful connection between the poem and the first and last rungs of the ladder.

The Animal Band *(cont.)*

Open Word Sort

1. Distribute sets of *The Animal Band Open Word Sort* cards (pages 103–104) to individual students, pairs of students, or groups of students.
2. Have students read the words and decide how they can be sorted.
3. Follow the sorting with a discussion of word meanings and reasons for how words were sorted.
4. Relate the words to the rhyme.

Rhyming Riddles 

1. Ask students to think of as many words that rhyme with the word *band* as they can. Have them share their words with partners.
2. Record their words on the board.
3. Distribute *The Animal Band Rhyming Riddles* (page 105) to students and make connections between the words students come up with in Step 1 with words in the Word Bank.
4. Instruct students to use words from the Word Bank to complete the riddles. Tell them that they will not use one of the words.
5. Have students illustrate one of the rhyming riddles on the backs of their papers.

Writing Connection 

1. Have students work in pairs to create two-column lists with names of animals in the first column, and sounds they make in the second column. **Note:** You may wish to have students use the Internet to find the animals and their sounds.
2. Have students share their lists with the class.
3. Count how many different animals were listed.

Reader's Theater 

1. Distribute *The Animal Band Reader's Theater* script (page 106) to students.
2. Divide the class into four groups.
3. Assign a stanza to each group.
4. Allow several rehearsals to develop fluency. Encourage groups to add voice effects as appropriate (e.g., for the word *high* use a high tone; for the word *deep* use a low tone).
5. Perform the reader's theater for the class, another class, or for a special school event.

The Animal Band

by Karen McGuigan Brothers

The cat sang high,
the dog sang deep,
the little chicks
sang, "Peep, peep, peep."

And right on cue
the cow said, "Moo,"
the sheep chimed in
a "Baa" or two.

The birds all sang
from on the roof,
the horse stomped time
with his big hoof.

They played for hours
and it was grand
to listen to
the animal band.

Name: ____________________

The Animal Band

Word Ladder

Directions: Listen to the clues. Then, write the words on the rungs below as you climb the ladder.

6. grand

5.

4.

3.

2.

1. band

The Animal Band

Open Word Sort

Directions: Cut apart the cards. Then, sort them into groups that you choose. Be ready to explain your groups.

animal	cat
dog	chicks
cow	sheep
birds	horse
peep	sang

The Animal Band

Open Word Sort *(cont.)*

moo	baa
said	chimed
stomped	played
listen	

Name: ______________________________

The Animal Band

Rhyming Riddles

Directions: Use words from the Word Bank to complete the riddles about animals. **Note:** You will not use one of the words.

Word Bank

errand sand band land grand understand

1. animals at the beach
   ____
   animals playing in the ______________

2. animals on a short trip to get something
   ____
   animals running an ______________

3. animals that are not in the sea
   ____
   animals that live on ______________

4. animals that are great
   ____
   animals that are ______________

5. animals making music
   ____
   animals in a ______________

The Animal Band

Reader's Theater

All: The Animal Band

Group 1: The cat sang high,
the dog sang deep,
the little chicks
sang, "Peep, peep,
peep."

Group 2: And right on cue
the cow said, "Moo,"
the sheep chimed in
a "Baa" or two.

Group 3: The birds all sang
from on the roof,
the horse stomped time
with his big hoof.

Group 4: They played for hours
and it was grand
to listen to
the animal band.

If I Could Live in a Dollhouse

Standards

- Know the spelling-sound correspondences for common consonant digraphs.
- Know final *-e* and common vowel team conventions for representing long vowel sounds.
- Recognize and read grade-appropriate irregularly spelled words.
- Describe people, places, things and events with relevant details, expressing ideas and feelings clearly.
- Produce and expand complete simple and compound declarative, interrogative, imperative, and exclamatory sentences in response to prompts.
- See Appendix C for additional standards.

Materials

- *If I Could Live in a Dollhouse* (page 109)
- *Letter Cards* (page 134)
- *If I Could Live in a Dollhouse Closed Word Sort* (pages 110–111)
- *If I Could Live in a Dollhouse Rhyming Riddles* (page 112)
- *If I Could Live in a Dollhouse Reader's Theater* (pages 113–114)

Procedures

Introducing the Rhyme

1. Tell students to close their eyes and make a mental picture of what is happening in a poem they are about to hear.
2. Read the poem to the class.
3. Have students open their eyes and share their images with partners.
4. Distribute the *If I Could Live in a Dollhouse* rhyme (page 109) to students.
5. Read the rhyme chorally several times to develop fluency.
6. Allow students to illustrate the rhyme and add it to their individual poetry notebooks.
7. Have students add the title to their notebooks' tables of contents.

Change a Word

1. Distribute a set of *Letter Cards* (page 134) to each student. If this activity is used early in the year, we recommend you use only the letters they will need (*a, d, e, h, i, n, o, o, l, l, r, s, t, t, y, y*).
2. Before you begin to play Change a Word, have students identify the letters and corresponding sounds.
3. Allow students time to arrange the letters to make their own words.
4. After students have had time to make and share words, ask them to put the letters in a pile and follow your instructions to make a word chain from *doll* to *dollhouse* (*doll-little-eat-tiny-yard-dollhouse*). Say the following:
   - We are going to make a chain of words. What kind of house is this poem about? Use four letters. What word did you make? (Write *doll* on the board.)
   - Use the last letter of *doll* to make a word that is a synonym for *tiny*. What word did you make? (Write *little* on the board.)
   - Use the last letter of *little* to make the word for what the author of the poem wants to do at the tiny table. What word did you make? (Write *eat* on the board.)

If I Could Live in a Dollhouse *(cont.)*

Change a Word *(cont.)*

- Use the last letter of *eat* to make the word for the size of everything in the dollhouse. What word did you make? (Write *tiny* on the board.)
- Use the last letter of *tiny* to make the word for the ground surrounding the tiny house. What word did you make? (Write *yard* on the board.)
- Use the last letter of *yard* to make the compound word that tells what kind of house is in the poem. What word did you make? (Write *dollhouse* on the board.)

Closed Word Sort

1. Distribute sets of the *If I Could Live in a Dollhouse Closed Word Sort* cards (pages 110–111) to individual students, pairs of students, or groups of students.
2. Introduce or review the term *syllables* with the class.
3. Ask students to put words into groups according to the number of syllables.
4. Follow the sorting by reading the words and discussing the syllables.
5. Relate the words to the rhyme.

Rhyming Riddles

1. Ask students to think of as many words that rhyme with the word *doll* as they can. Have them share their words with partners.
2. Record their words on the board.
3. Distribute *If I Could Live in a Dollhouse Rhyming Riddles* (page 112) to students and make connections between the words students come up with in Step 1 with the words in the Word Bank.
4. Instruct students to use words from the Word Bank to complete the riddles. Tell them that they will not use one of the words.
5. Have students illustrate one of the rhyming riddles on the backs of their papers.

Writing Connection

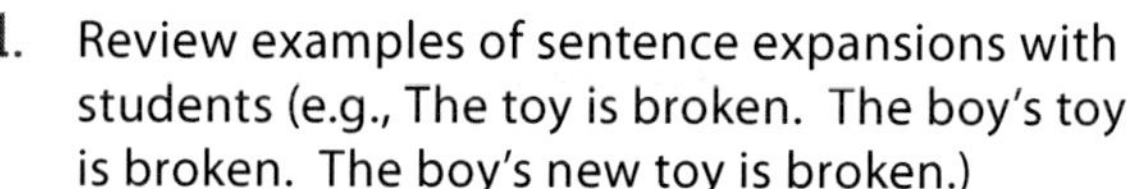

1. Review examples of sentence expansions with students (e.g., The toy is broken. The boy's toy is broken. The boy's new toy is broken.)
2. Write several simple sentences on the board, and ask students to expand them.
3. Write the following sentence related to the poem on the board: *The dollhouse is tiny.*
4. Have students work with partners to expand the sentence.
5. Allow students to share their expanded sentences.

Reader's Theater

1. Distribute the *If I Could Live in a Dollhouse Reader's Theater* script (pages 113–114) to students.
2. Have students read the script independently.
3. Discuss the script.
4. Assign parts for five readers.
5. Allow several rehearsals to develop fluency.
6. Perform the reader's theater for the class, another class, or for a special school event.

If I Could Live in a Dollhouse

by Karen McGuigan Brothers

If I could live in a dollhouse
I'd sit in a tiny chair
pulled up to a tiny table
shaped like a tiny square.

I'd cook in a tiny skillet
on top of a tiny range;
To be so very tiny
would be so very strange.

I'd take a tiny nap
upon a tiny bed
and dream a tiny dream
inside my tiny head.

I'd take a tiny book
down from a tiny shelf
and read a tiny story
all by my tiny self.

I'd hang up tiny curtains
and decorate with pride.
That's what I'd do in a dollhouse
If I could live inside.

If I Could Live in a Dollhouse

Closed Word Sort

Directions: Cut apart the cards. Then, sort them into groups that have the same number of syllables.

I	range
live	nap
square	chair
pride	tiny

If I Could Live in a Dollhouse

Closed Word Sort *(cont.)*

skillet	upon
bed	dream
book	dollhouse
inside	decorate

Name: ______________________________

If I Could Live in a Dollhouse

Rhyming Riddles

Directions: Use words from the Word Bank to complete the riddles about dolls. **Note:** You will not use one of the words.

Word Bank

hall	fall	tall	wall	call	mall

1. a doll that is shopping

   a doll at the ______________

2. a doll that could get hurt

   a doll that might ______________

3. a doll that is as big as a father

   a doll that is ______________

4. a doll that is on the phone

   a doll making a ______________

5. a picture of a doll

   a doll on the ______________

If I Could Live in a Dollhouse

Reader's Theater

All: If I Could Live in a Dollhouse

Reader 1: I think it would be fun to be that small.

Reader 2: It would be okay as long as you were in the dollhouse.

Reader 3: Why?

Reader 2: Because if you came out, you would have to be afraid that someone would step on you.

Reader 4: You would also have to be afraid of bugs. Even a fly would look really big.

Reader 5: But maybe you could get a ride on a butterfly.

Reader 1: That would be fun.

Reader 2: I think it would be okay as long as you had some really small friends you could hang out with.

Reader 3: Yes, but you would miss hanging out with your family.

Reader 4: You could not go anywhere with your family unless people carried you in their pockets.

If I Could Live in a Dollhouse

Reader's Theater *(cont.)*

Reader 5: I think it is fun to think about how it would be to live in a dollhouse, but I would not really want to do it.

Reader 1: I think it is fun to think about how it would be to live in a submarine under the sea, but I would not really want to do that either.

Reader 2: I like it just fine being the size I am and living where I live.

All: Me, too.

It's Raining, It's Pouring

Standards

- Read words with inflectional endings.
- Identify frequently occurring root words and their inflectional forms.
- Know final *-e* and common vowel team conventions for representing long vowel sounds.
- Use frequently occurring adjectives.
- See Appendix C for additional standards.

Materials

- *It's Raining, It's Pouring* (page 117)
- *It's Raining, It's Pouring Word Ladder* (page 118)
- *It's Raining, It's Pouring Closed Word Sort* (pages 119–120)
- *It's Raining, It's Pouring Rhyming Riddles* (page 121)
- *It's Raining, It's Pouring Reader's Theater* (pages 122–123)

Procedures

Introducing the Rhyme

1. Distribute the *It's Raining, It's Pouring* rhyme (page 117) to students.
2. Many of your students may know this rhyme and be able to recite it without the text. In order to encourage students to track print, divide the class into five groups and ask them to read their lines as indicated below. Instruct them to follow the print so that the reading is fluent, as if one voice were reading the entire rhyme.

   Group 1: It's raining,

   Group 2: It's pouring,

   Group 3: The old man is snoring;

   Group 4: He went to bed

   Group 5: and bumped his head

   All: And couldn't get up in the morning.
3. Read the rhyme several times to develop fluency.
4. Allow students to illustrate the rhyme and add it to their individual poetry notebooks.
5. Have students add the title to their notebooks' tables of contents.

Word Ladder

1. Distribute *It's Raining, It's Pouring Word Ladder* (page 118) to students.
2. Allow students time to observe the illustrations on their activity sheets.
3. After students have had time to review their activity sheets, tell them to follow your clues to make a word ladder from *man* to *snore*. Say the following:
   - start at the bottom of the ladder—The person in the rhyme was an old ______. (*man*)
   - add a letter to the end—This surrounds a lion's face. (*mane*)
   - change one letter—a female horse (*mare*)
   - replace the first letter with two different letters—This is what friends do with objects they have. (*share*)
   - change one of the vowels—This borders a large body of water such as an ocean. (*shore*)
   - change the beginning sound—what the old man does (*snore*)
4. Help students make a meaningful connection between the poem and the first and last rungs of the ladder.

It's Raining, It's Pouring *(cont.)*

Closed Word Sort

1. Distribute sets of the *It's Raining, It's Pouring Closed Word Sort* cards (pages 119–120) to individual students, pairs of students, or groups of students.
2. Review with students what verb tenses are.
3. Ask students to put words into groups according to the verb tense (e.g., happening right now, continuing to happen, happened in the past).
4. Follow the sorting by reading the words and discussing the verb forms.
5. Relate the words to the rhyme.

Rhyming Riddles 

1. Ask students to think of as many words that rhyme with the word *rain* as they can. Have them share their words with partners.
2. Record their words on the board.
3. Distribute *It's Raining, It's Pouring Rhyming Riddles* (page 121) to students and make connections between the words students come up with in Step 1 with the words in the Word Bank.
4. Instruct students to use words from the Word Bank to complete the riddles. Tell them that they will not use one of the words.
5. Have students illustrate one of the rhyming riddles on the backs of their papers.

Writing Connection 

1. Have students brainstorm lists of adjectives to pair with the word *man* (e.g., old man, snoring man, sleepy man).
2. Have students share their lists with the class.

Reader's Theater 

1. Distribute the *It's Raining, It's Pouring Reader's Theater* script (pages 122–123) to students.
2. Assign parts for five readers.
3. Allow several rehearsals to develop fluency.
4. Perform the reader's theater for the class, another class, or for a special school event.

It's Raining, It's Pouring

Traditional Rhyme

It's raining, it's pouring,
The old man is snoring.
He went to bed and
bumped his head
And couldn't get up in
the morning.

Name: ________________________________

It's Raining, It's Pouring

Word Ladder

Directions: Listen to the clues. Then, write the words on the rungs below as you climb the ladder.

6. snore

5.

4.

3.

2.

1. man

It's Raining, It's Pouring

Closed Word Sort

Directions: Cut apart the cards. Then, sort them according to whether the action is happening right now, is continuing to happen, or happened in the past.

rain	pouring
snore	raining
snored	bumped
snoring	bumping
snores	bumps

It's Raining, It's Pouring

Closed Word Sort *(cont.)*

rains	get
pours	getting
gets	

Name: ______________________________

It's Raining, It's Pouring

Rhyming Riddles

Directions: Use words from the Word Bank to complete the riddles about rain. **Note:** You will not use one of the words.

Word Bank

train	pain	drain	grain	stain	brain

1. rain that blows hard and stings your face

   ____

   rain that causes ______________________

2. rain that falls on a choo-choo

   ____

   rain falling on a ______________________

3. rain that falls on wheat fields

   ____

   rain falling on ______________________

4. rain that goes down the gutter

   ____

   rain going down the ______________________

5. thinking about rain

   ____

   rain on the ______________________

It's Raining, It's Pouring

Reader's Theater

All: It's Raining, It's Pouring

All: It's raining, it's pouring,
The old man is snoring.
He went to bed and bumped his head
And couldn't get up in the morning.

Reader 1: That's a funny rhyme.

Reader 2: What do you mean?

Reader 3: I was just wondering what an old man snoring had to do with rain.

Reader 4: Maybe the sound of the rain put him to sleep.

Reader 5: Or maybe it's raining in the middle of the night when he's already in bed and asleep.

Reader 2: I wonder what he bumped his head on.

Reader 3: Maybe he bumped it on the headboard.

Reader 4: What's a headboard?

Reader 5: That's the top part of the bed that goes against the wall.

Reader 4: Do you think he got hurt?

Reader 3: Maybe he knocked himself out and that's why he couldn't get up.

It's Raining, It's Pouring

Reader's Theater *(cont.)*

Reader 2: But the rhyme said he was snoring. I don't think people who are knocked out snore.

Reader 4: My grandpa snores.

Reader 5: So does my dad.

Reader 3: My mom snores, too, but she said not to tell anyone.

Reader 4: Now I'm worried about the old man because he couldn't get up in the morning.

Reader 1: I think we should change the last line.

Reader 2: To what?

Reader 3: I know. We should change it to "but he was okay in the morning."

Reader 1: Okay. Let's say the rhyme again with the new ending.

All: It's raining, it's pouring,
The old man is snoring.
He went to bed and bumped his head
But he was okay in the morning.

Reader 1: I like it.

All: Me, too.

I Eat My Peas with Honey

Standards

- Know final *-e* and common vowel team conventions for representing long vowel sounds.
- Recognize and read grade-appropriate irregularly spelled words.
- See Appendix C for additional standards.

Materials

- *I Eat My Peas with Honey* (page 126)
- *I Eat My Peas with Honey Word Ladder* (page 127)
- *I Eat My Peas with Honey Closed Word Sort* (page 128)
- *I Eat My Peas with Honey Rhyming Riddles* (page 129)
- *I Eat My Peas with Honey Reader's Theater* (pages 130–131)

Procedures

Introducing the Rhyme

1. Distribute the *I Eat My Peas with Honey* rhyme (page 126) to students.
2. Divide students into pairs. Have students practice reading the rhyme.
3. Have each student pair think of a character, and have them practice reading the poem in the voice that character might use. Encourage them to also use actions that represent the character (e.g., sleepy, cowboy, superhero).
4. Share readings with the class.
5. Allow students to illustrate the rhyme and add it to their individual poetry notebooks.
6. Have students add the title to their notebooks' tables of contents.

Word Ladder

1. Distribute *I Eat My Peas with Honey Word Ladder* (page 127) to students.
2. Allow students time to observe the illustrations on their activity sheets.
3. After students have had time to review their activity sheets, tell them to follow your clues to make a word ladder from *eat* to *peas*. Say the following:
   - start at the bottom of the ladder—what the person in the poem does at dinnertime (*eat*)
   - add one letter—what you do when you win a race, or what you do with a drum (*beat*)
   - change the first letter—what you sit on (*seat*)
   - add one letter—make number 3 plural (*seats*)
   - remove one letter—another word for oceans (*seas*)
   - change one letter—what the person in the poem eats (*peas*)
4. Help students make a meaningful connection between the poem and the first and last rungs of the ladder.

I Eat My Peas with Honey *(cont.)*

Closed Word Sort 

1. Distribute sets of the *I Eat My Peas with Honey Closed Word Sort* cards (page 128) to individual students, pairs of students, or groups of students.
2. Review with students the long ē vowel rules.
3. Ask students to put words into groups according to the long ē vowel rules.
4. Follow the sorting by reading the words and discussing the vowel rules.
5. Relate the words to the rhyme.

Rhyming Riddles 

1. Ask students to think of as many words with the /ē/ sound as in *pea* as they can. Have them share their words with partners.
2. Record their words on the board.
3. Distribute *I Eat My Peas with Honey Rhyming Riddles* (page 129) to students and make connections between the words students come up with in Step 1 with the words in the Word Bank.
4. Instruct students to use words from the Word Bank to complete the riddles. Tell them that they will not use one of the words.
5. Have students illustrate one of the rhyming riddles on the backs of their papers.

Writing Connection 

1. Have students divide their writing paper lengthwise to create two columns.
2. Label the left side *Foods I Love*, and label the right side *Foods I Try to Avoid*.
3. Have students fill both columns.
4. Allow students to share their lists with partners.

Reader's Theater 

1. Distribute the *I Eat My Peas with Honey Reader's Theater Script* (pages 130–131) to students.
2. Assign parts for five readers.
3. Allow several rehearsals to develop fluency.
4. Perform the reader's theater for the class, another class, or for a special school event.

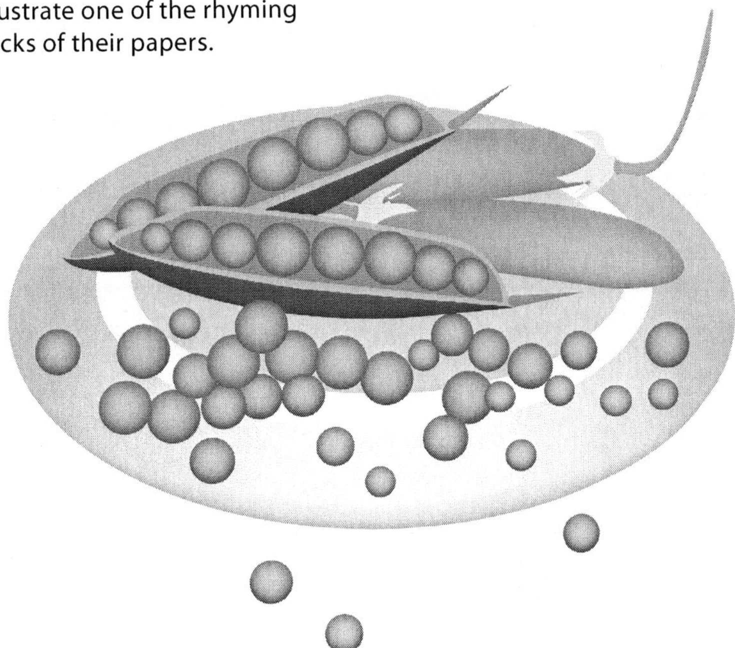

I Eat My Peas with Honey

Traditional Rhyme

I eat my peas with honey,
I've done it all my life;
It makes the peas
taste funny,
But it keeps them on
my knife.

Name: ______________________________

I Eat My Peas with Honey

Word Ladder

Directions: Listen to the clues. Then, write the words on the rungs below as you climb the ladder.

6. peas

5.

4.

3.

2.

1. eat

I Eat My Peas with Honey

Closed Word Sort

Directions: Cut apart the cards. Then, sort them according to the long ē vowel rules.

eat	beans
keeps	bunny
see	sea
beat	mean
monkey	donkey
baby	happy
daddy	money

Name: ______________________________

I Eat My Peas with Honey

Rhyming Riddles

Directions: Use words from the Word Bank to complete the riddles about peas. **Note:** You will not use one of the words.

Word Bank

seat	meat	sea	keep	read	tree

1. peas hanging from branches

   peas in a ______________

2. peas in a chair

   peas in a ______________

3. peas in a large body of water

   peas in the ______________

4. peas with books

   peas that can ______________

5. peas that we want to save

   peas we will ______________

I Eat My Peas with Honey

Reader's Theater

All: I Eat My Peas with Honey

All: I eat my peas with honey,
I've done it all my life.
It makes the peas taste funny,
But it keeps them on my knife.

Reader 1: Yuck! Who would eat their peas with honey?

Reader 2: That would make me sick!

Reader 3: Me, too.

Reader 4: Honey is good on toast.

Reader 5: I like honey with peanut butter on a sandwich.

Reader 2: My dad likes bananas on his peanut butter sandwich.

Reader 1: Yuck! That sounds bad, too.

Reader 3: At least the person in the poem had a reason for eating peas with honey.

Reader 4: He ate them that way to keep them on his knife.

Reader 5: Why would he eat them with a knife?

I Eat My Peas with Honey

Reader's Theater (cont.)

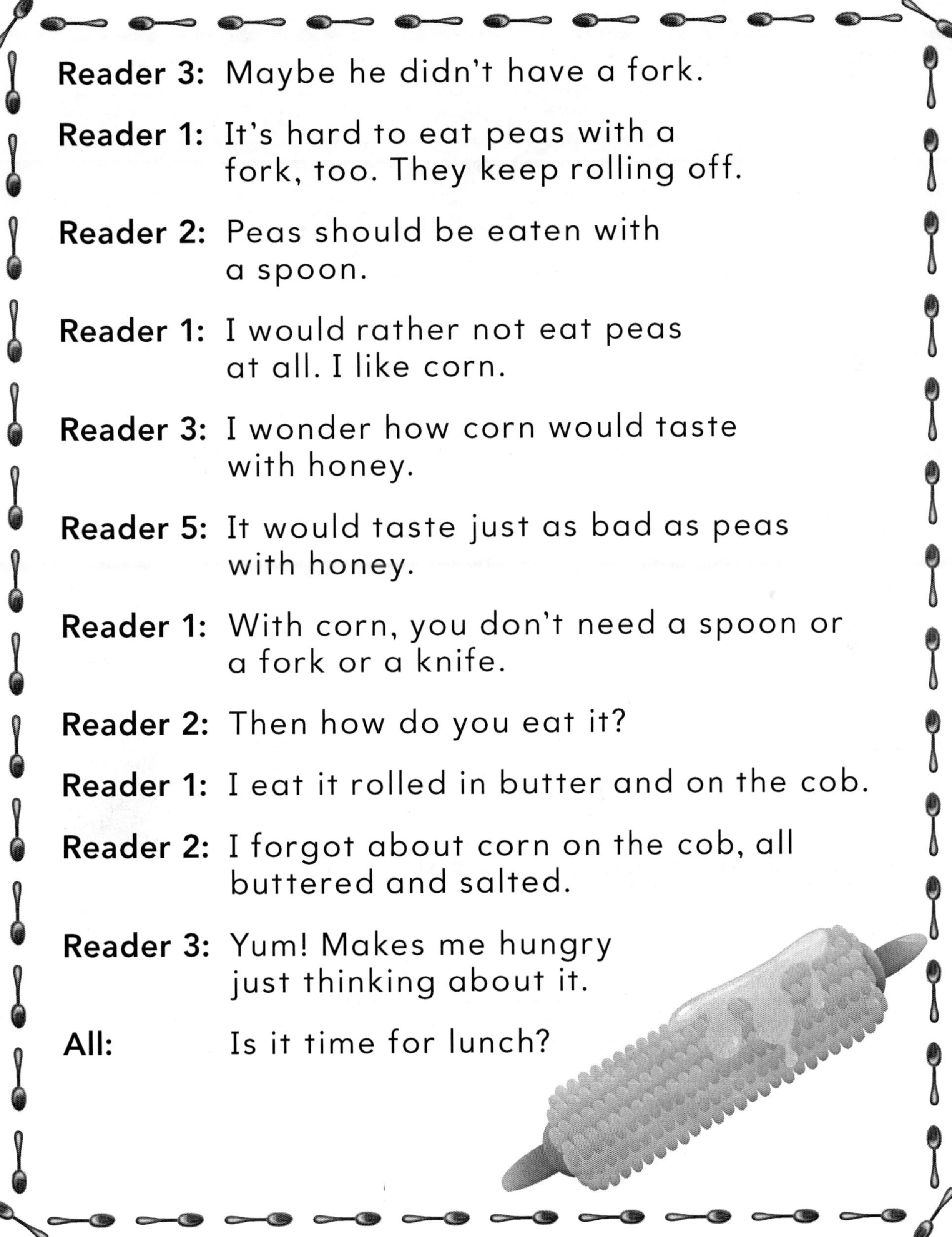

Reader 3: Maybe he didn't have a fork.

Reader 1: It's hard to eat peas with a fork, too. They keep rolling off.

Reader 2: Peas should be eaten with a spoon.

Reader 1: I would rather not eat peas at all. I like corn.

Reader 3: I wonder how corn would taste with honey.

Reader 5: It would taste just as bad as peas with honey.

Reader 1: With corn, you don't need a spoon or a fork or a knife.

Reader 2: Then how do you eat it?

Reader 1: I eat it rolled in butter and on the cob.

Reader 2: I forgot about corn on the cob, all buttered and salted.

Reader 3: Yum! Makes me hungry just thinking about it.

All: Is it time for lunch?

Tips for Implementing the Lessons

The Importance of Routines

Reading instruction needs to include a measure of predictability through activities that students do at regular times in their language arts classroom. Routines allow students to become self-directed learners because once they learn the routine, they do not have to rely on the teacher for directions for what to do next. This increases students' learning time and decreases teachers' planning time (Rasinski and Padak 2013; Rasinski, Padak, and Fawcett 2010).

Each lesson in this book follows a routine:

1. Introduction, Reading, and Rereading of the Rhyme
2. Word Work activities
   - ➔ *Word Ladder* or *Change a Word*
   - ➔ *Word Sort*
   - ➔ *Rhyming Riddles*
3. Writing Connection
4. Reader's Theater

The intention is not that you march sequentially through all the rhymes and activities in this book. Use the standards that accompany each lesson to guide you in selecting the rhymes and activities that your students need at any given time. Some standards may be addressed adequately in other instructional materials you use, while you may find some gaps in your curriculum that can be filled with activities in this book. In addition to the standards, stay attuned to what your students enjoy and learn from most.

Each lesson has multiple activities, so even if you eliminate a few, you will not be able to complete an entire lesson in one day. The following one-week routine can be adjusted according to the number of activities you decide to use. Another option is to learn the rhymes early in the year, revisit them regularly, and do an activity each time you revisit them.

Day	Task
Day 1	Introduce the rhyme to students.
Day 2	Reread the rhyme and complete one of the word work activities.
Day 3	Assign and practice the reader's theater script and complete a second word work activity.
Day 4	Practice the reader's theater script and complete the last word work activity.
Day 5	Perform the reader's theater script and complete the writing connection activity.

Tips for Implementing the Lessons *(cont.)*

Differentiation

We have been in education long enough to know that, despite frequent attempts at standardizing curriculum, instruction, and assessment, there is no such thing as a "standardized" child. Children in our schools come with great differences in abilities, background experiences, and motivation to learn.

Each lesson begins with the class orally reading a rhyme or poem. Early in the year some of your students may not have the word attack skills to read the rhymes independently. Choral reading will allow the more fluent readers to provide support for their less fluent classmates. It is a wonderful way to build group spirit and cohesion. Don't worry if some students seem to be "memorizing" rather than actually reading the words. Although in past years students were discouraged from using their fingers to point to words, we now know this is an appropriate strategy for children just learning to read, so encourage students to track print with their fingers, and before long the memorized words will become part of their reading vocabulary.

Your students may be familiar with many of the rhymes already. In that case, you will find the reader's theater scripts a good extension of the rhymes as well as an excellent source of reading material.

As with any instructional material, there is no one thing in this book that will work for all children all the time. Your professional knowledge and experience will guide you in selecting which parts of the lessons you should use.

Poetry Notebooks

Poetry Notebooks are an effective and engaging way to help students learn to recognize the form and sound of poetry. After the initial introduction of a poem or rhyme, students are given copies of it that they illustrate and add to three-ring binders.

Throughout the year, students enjoy browsing their poetry notebooks during sustained silent reading, reading poems with a partner during independent reading time, and sharing the poems with family and friends. A table of contents will help students locate their favorites. Some teachers add a "Lucky Listener" sheet to the front of the poetry notebook. Students take the notebooks home on a regular basis, and anyone they read to signs the sheet and makes comments if they wish. Some children even read to their pets and sign it themselves ("Good job! Love, Goldie") or make a paw print in the signature space. To help your students create poetry notebooks, see pages 136–138 for the *My Poetry Notebook* cover, the *Table of Contents*, and the *Lucky Listener* page.

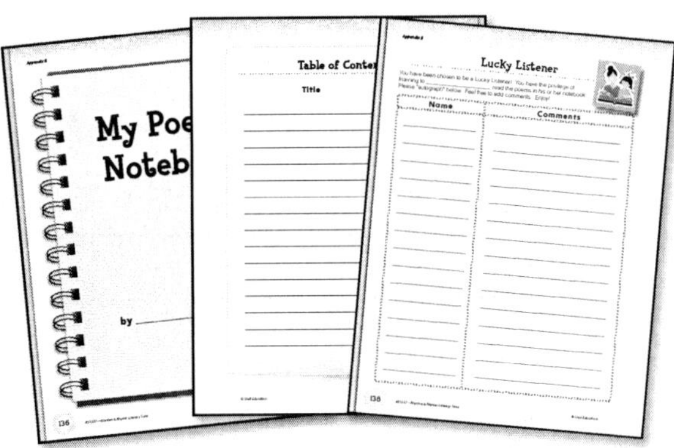

Letter Cards

Teacher Directions: Copy and cut apart the cards. Distribute sets to students. **Note:** Read Step 1 in all *Change a Word* activities to see if you need to write additional letters on the empty cards.

a	b	c	d	e
f	g	h	i	j
k	l	m	n	o
p	q	r	s	t
u	v	w	x	y
z				

Name: ______________________________

My Rhyming Words

Words that rhyme with ______________

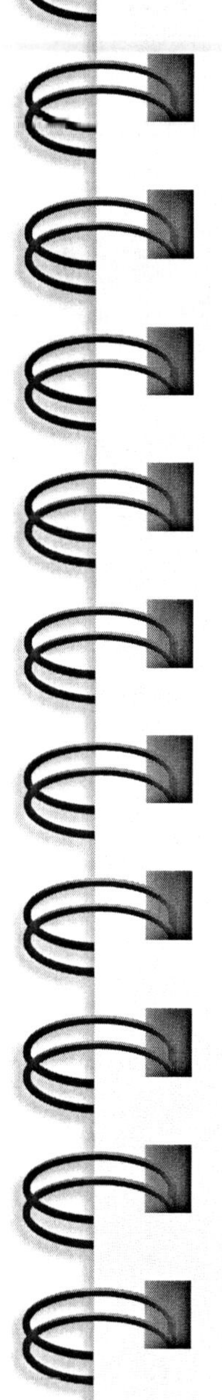

My Poetry Notebook

by ______________________________

Table of Contents

Title	Page

Lucky Listener

You have been chosen to be a Lucky Listener! You have the privilege of listening to ____________________ read the poems in his or her notebook. Please "autograph" below. Feel free to add comments. Enjoy!

Name	Comments

Standards Correlations

Shell Education is committed to producing educational materials that are research and standards based. In this effort, we have correlated all of our products to the academic standards of all 50 states, the District of Columbia, the Department of Defense Dependents Schools, and all Canadian provinces.

How to Find Standards Correlations

To print a customized correlation report of this product for your state, visit our website at http://www.shelleducation.com and follow the on-screen directions. If you require assistance in printing correlation reports, please contact our Customer Service Department at 1-877-777-3450.

Purpose and Intent of Standards

Legislation mandates that all states adopt academic standards that identify the skills students will learn in kindergarten through grade twelve. Many states also have standards for Pre–K. This same legislation sets requirements to ensure the standards are detailed and comprehensive.

Standards are designed to focus instruction and guide adoption of curricula. Standards are statements that describe the criteria necessary for students to meet specific academic goals. They define the knowledge, skills, and content students should acquire at each level. Standards are also used to develop standardized tests to evaluate students' academic progress. Teachers are required to demonstrate how their lessons meet state standards. State standards are used in the development of all of our products, so educators can be assured they meet the academic requirements of each state.

Common Core State Standards

The activities in this book are aligned to the Common Core State Standards (CCSS). The chart on pages 140–142 lists the standards addressed in each lesson. Specific standards are also listed on the first page of each lesson.

TESOL and WIDA Standards

The activities in this book promote English language development for English language learners. The following TESOL and WIDA standards are addressed through the activities in this book:

- **Standard 1:** English language learners **communicate** for **social**, **intercultural**, and **instructional** purposes within the school setting.
- **Standard 2:** English language learners **communicate** information, ideas, and concepts necessary for academic success in the area of **language arts**.

Standards Correlations *(cont.)*

Standards that are specific to lessons are included on the first pages of the lessons and in the chart below. Standards that fit every lesson are listed below and indicate All Lessons. They are not always indicated on the first pages of the lessons.

Standards	Lessons
Literacy.L.1.1.c—Use singular and plural nouns with matching verbs in basic sentences.	There Was an Old Woman Who Lived in a Shoe (p. 48); Humpty Dumpty (p. 82)
Literacy.L.1.1.f—Use frequently occurring adjectives.	Rubber Duck (p. 64); Apples (p. 92); It's Raining, It's Pouring (p. 115)
Literacy.L.1.1.j—Produce and expand complete simple and compound declarative, interrogative, imperative, and exclamatory sentences in response to prompts.	There Was an Old Woman Who Lived in a Shoe (p. 48); If I Could Live in a Dollhouse (p. 107)
Literacy.L.1.2—Demonstrate command of the conventions of standard English grammar and usage when writing or speaking.	All Lessons
Literacy.L.1.2.b—Use end punctuation for sentences.	Hey Diddle Diddle (p. 15); Peter, Peter, Pumpkin Eater (p. 39); There Was an Old Woman Who Lived in a Shoe (p. 48); If I Could Live in a Dollhouse (p. 107)
Literacy.L.1.2.d—Use conventional spelling for words with common spelling patterns and for frequently occurring irregular words.	All Lessons
Literacy.L.1.2.e—Spell untaught words phonetically, drawing on phonemic awareness and spelling conventions.	All Lessons
Literacy.L.1.4.c—Identify frequently occurring root words and their inflectional forms.	It's Raining, It's Pouring (p. 115)
Literacy.L.1.5.a—Sort words into categories (e.g., colors, clothing) to gain a sense of the concepts the categories represent.	All Lessons
Literacy.L.1.6—Use words and phrases acquired through conversations, reading and being read to, and responding to texts, including using adjectives and adverbs to describe.	Fireflies (p. 57); Humpty Dumpty (p. 82)
Literacy.L.2.1.e—Use adjectives and adverbs, and choose between them depending on what is to be modified. (grade 2)	Fireflies (p. 57)

Standards Correlations *(cont.)*

Standards	Lessons
Literacy.RF.1.2—Demonstrate understanding of spoken words, syllables, and sounds.	Fuzzy Wuzzy (p. 24)
Literacy.RF.1.2.a—Distinguish long from short vowel sounds in spoken single-syllable words.	Apples (p. 92)
Literacy.RF.1.3—Know and apply grade-level phonics and word analysis skills in decoding words.	All Lessons
Literacy.RF.1.3.a—Know the spelling-sound correspondences for common consonant digraphs.	Hey Diddle Diddle (p. 15); Apples (p. 92); If I Could Live in a Dollhouse (p. 107)
Literacy.RF.1.3.b—Decode regularly spelled one-syllable words.	All Lessons
Literacy.RF.1.3.c—Know final *-e* and common vowel team conventions for representing long vowel sounds.	Peter, Peter, Pumpkin Eater (p. 39); Apples (p. 92); If I Could Live in a Dollhouse (p. 107); It's Raining, It's Pouring (p. 115); I Eat My Peas with Honey (p. 124)
Literacy.RF.1.3.d—Use knowledge that every syllable must have a vowel sound to determine the number of syllables in a printed word.	Pretty Star (p. 32)
Literacy.RF.1.3.e—Decode two-syllable words following basic patterns by breaking the words into syllables.	Peter, Peter, Pumpkin Eater (p. 39)
Literacy.RF.1.3.f—Read words with inflectional endings.	It's Raining, It's Pouring (p. 115)
Literacy.RF.1.3.g—Recognize and read grade-appropriate irregularly spelled words.	Humpty Dumpty (p. 82); The Animal Band (p. 99); If I Could Live in a Dollhouse (p. 107); I Eat My Peas with Honey (p. 124)
Literacy.RF.1.4—Read with sufficient accuracy and fluency to support comprehension.	All Lessons
Literacy.RF.1.4.a—Read on-level text with purpose and understanding.	All Lessons
Literacy.RF.1.4.b—Read on-level text orally with accuracy, appropriate rate, and expression on successive readings.	All Lessons
Literacy.RF.1.4.c—Use context to confirm or self-correct word recognition and understanding, rereading as necessary.	All Lessons
Literacy.RI.1.5—Know and use various text features to locate key facts or information in a text.	Hop, Bunny, Hop (p. 9)
Literacy.RL.1.1—Ask and answer questions about key details in a text.	All Lessons

Standards Correlations *(cont.)*

Standards	Lessons
Literacy.RL.1.3—Describe characters, setting, and major events in a story, using key details.	All Lessons
Literacy.RL.1.4—Identify words and phrases in stories or poems that suggest feelings or appeal to the senses.	All Lessons
Literacy.RL.1.6—Identify who is telling the story at various points in a text.	Three Little Kittens (p. 73)
Literacy.RL.1.7—Use illustrations and details in a story to describe its characters, setting, or events.	Hey Diddle Diddle (p. 15); Humpty Dumpty (p. 82)
Literacy.RL.1.10—With prompting and support, read prose and poetry of appropriate complexity for grade 1.	All Lessons
Literacy.SL.1.3—Ask and answer questions about what a speaker says in order to gather additional information or clarify something that is not understood.	All Lessons
Literacy.SL.1.4—Describe people, places, things, and events with relevant details, expressing ideas and feelings clearly.	If I Could Live in a Dollhouse (p. 107)
Literacy.SL.1.5—Produce complete sentences when appropriate to task and situation.	All Lessons
Literacy.W.1.3—Write narratives in which they recount a well-elaborated event or short sequence of events. Include details to describe actions, thoughts, and feelings, use temporal words to signal event order, and provide a sense of closure.	Fuzzy Wuzzy (p. 24); Humpty Dumpty (p. 82)
Literacy.W.1.5—With guidance and support from adults, focus on a topic, respond to questions and suggestions from peers, and add details to strengthen writing as needed.	All Lessons
Literacy.W.1.6—With guidance and support from adults, use a variety of digital tools to produce and publish writing, including in collaboration with peers.	The Animal Band (p. 99)

References Cited

Adams, Marilyn J. 1990. Beginning to Read: Thinking and learning about print. Cambridge, MA: MIT Press.

Ball, Eileen, and Benita A. Blachman. 1991. Does Phoneme Awareness Training in Kindergarten Make a Difference in Early Word Recognition and Developmental Spelling? *Reading Research Quarterly* 26: 49–66.

Bromley, Karen. 2007. Nine Things Every Teacher Should Know About Words and Vocabulary Instruction. *Journal of Adolescent and Adult Literacy* 50: 528–537.

Bryant, Peter E., Lynette Bradley, Morag Maclean, and Jennifer Crossland. 1989. Nursery Rhymes, Phonological Skills, and Reading. *Journal of Child Language* 16 (2): 407–428.

Chall, Jeanne. 1983. *Stages of Reading Development*. New York, NY: McGraw Hill.

Denman, Gregory A. 1988. *When You've Made it Your Own: Teaching Poetry to Young People.* Portsmouth, NH: Heinemann.

Dowhower, Sarah L. 1987. Effects of Repeated Reading on Second-Grade Transitional Readers' Fluency and Comprehension. *Reading Research Quarterly* 22: 389–407.

———. 1997. The Method of Repeated Readings. *The Reading Teacher* 50: 376.

Dunst, Carl, Diana Meter, and Deborah W. Hornby. 2011. Relationship Between Young Children's Nursery Rhyme Experiences and Knowledge and Phonological and Print-Related Abilities. *Center for Early Literacy Learning* 4: 1–12.

Gill, Sharon R. 2011. The Forgotten Genre of Children's Poetry. *The Reading Teacher* 60: 622–625.

Griffith, Priscilla L., and Janell P. Klesius. 1990. The Effect of Phonemic Awareness Ability and Reading Instructional Approach on First Grade Children's Acquisition of Spelling and Decoding Skills. Paper presented at the annual meeting of the National Reading Conference, Miami, FL.

Hackett, Kelly. 2013. *Ready! Set! Go! Literacy Centers*. Huntington Beach, CA: Shell Publishing.

Iwasaki, Becky, Timothy V. Rasinski, Kasim Yildirim, and Belinda S. Zimmerman. 2013. Let's Bring Back the Magic of Song for Teaching Reading. *The Reading Teacher* 67: 137–141.

Maclean, Morag, Peter Bryant, and Lynette Bradley. 1987. Rhymes, Nursery Rhymes, and Reading in Early Childhood. *Merrill Palmer Quarterly* 33: 255–281.

National Reading Panel. 2000. Report of the National Reading Panel: Teaching Children to Read. Report of the subgroups. Washington, DC: U.S. Department of Health and Human Services, National Institutes of Health.

Perfect, Kathy A. 1999. "Rhyme and Reason: Poetry for the Heart and Head." *The Reading Teacher,* 5: 728–737.

Rasinski, Timothy V., and Nancy D. Padak. 2013. *From Phonics to Fluency: Effective Teaching of Decoding and Reading Fluency in the Elementary School.* Boston, MA: Pearson.

References Cited *(cont.)*

Rasinski, Timothy V., Nancy D. Padak, and Gay Fawcett. 2010. *Teaching Children Who Find Reading Difficult, 4th ed.* Boston, MA: Pearson.

Rasinski, Timothy V., Nancy D. Padak, Elizabeth Sturtevant, and Wayne Linek. 1994. "Effects of Fluency Development on Urban Second-Grade Readers." *Journal of Educational Research* 87: 158–165.

Rasinski, Timothy V., William H. Rupley, and William D. Nichols. 2008. Two Essential Ingredients: Phonics and Fluency Getting to Know Each Other." *The Reading Teacher* 62: 257–260.

———. 2012. *Phonics and Fluency Practice with Poetry.* New York: Scholastic.

Rasinski, Timothy V., and Belinda Zimmerman. 2013. What's the Perfect Text for Struggling Readers? Try Poetry! *Reading Today* 30: 15–16.

Samuels, S. Jay. 1997. The Method of Repeated Readings. *The Reading Teacher* 50: 376–381.

Seitz, Sheila K. 2013. "Poetic Fluency." *The Reading Teacher* 67: 312–14.

Stahl, Steven A. 2003. "Vocabulary and Readability: How Knowing Word Meanings Affects Comprehension." *Topics in Language Disorders* 23 (3): 241–248.

Stahl, Steven A., and Kathleen M. Heubach. 2005. "Fluency-Oriented Reading Instruction." *Journal of Literacy Research* 37: 25–60.

Stanovich, Keith E. 1994. "Romance and Reason." *The Reading Teacher* 49: 280–291.

Templeton, Shane, and Donald Bear. 2011. Teaching Phonemic Awareness, Spelling, and Word Recognition. *In Rebuilding the Foundation: Effective Reading Instruction for the 21st Century,* edited by Timothy Rasinski 1–10. Bloomington, IN: Solution Tree.

Zimmerman, Belinda, and Timothy V. Rasinski. 2012. The Fluency Development Lesson: A Model of Authentic and Effective Fluency Instruction."*In Fluency Instruction* 2nd ed., edited by Timothy V. Rasinski, Camille Blachowicz, and Kristin Lems 172–184. New York, NY: Guilford.

Zimmerman, Belinda, Timothy V. Rasinski, and Maria Melewski. 2013. When Kids Can't Read, What a Focus on Fluency Can Do. *In Advanced Literacy Practices: From the Clinic to the Classroom,* edited by Evan Ortlieb and Earl H. Cheek 137–160. Bingley, UK: Emerald Group Publishing.